34.50
75E

RESPONSES OF JAMAICAN AND AMERICAN DEAF GROUPS TO STIGMA

A Critical Interpretive Approach

Jennifer Maria Keane-Dawes

University Press of America, Inc.
Lanham • New York • Oxford

Library of Congress Cataloging-in-Publication Data

Keane-Dawes, Jennifer Maria.
Responses of Jamaican and American deaf groups to stigma : a critical
interpretive approach / Jennifer Maria Keane-Dawes.
p.   cm.
Includes bibliographical references and index.
1. Deaf--Cross-Cultural studies. 2. Stigma (Social psychology)--
Cross-cultural studies. 4. Social adjustment--Cross-cultural studies. I.
Title.
HV2395.K43   1997 305.9'08162--dc21   96-50437 CIP

ISBN 0-7618-0652-0 (cloth: alk. ppr.)

HV 2395 .K43 1997

Keane-Dawes, Jennifer Maria.

Responses of Jamaican and
American deaf groups to

Dedication

To my six year old son, Thomas Jermaine Keane-Dawes,
The wind beneath my wings,
And to all mothers who rear their sons alone.

Acknowledgments

My thanks must first go to the Lord Jesus Christ, who kept his promise that "I the Lord thy God will hold thy right hand, saying unto thee, fear not. I will help thee." Isaiah 41:13.

To my "dream team" Dr. William Starosta, Dr. Melbourne Cummings, Dr. Lyndrey Niles, and Dr. Anne Nicotera, I give heartfelt thanks. Special appreciation is extended to Dr. William Starosta, my dissertation advisor. His was the door that was never closed to me, the mind that mentored me with the finest scholarship, and the voice that gave my idea research life. Dr. Melbourne Cummings was the creator of my opportunities. She believed in me even when I could not believe in myself. Dr. Lyndrey Niles, my friend, journeyed with me through the process and removed every major obstacle that confronted me. Unrelentingly thorough and analytic, Dr. Anne Nicotera's brilliance directed me to the light at the end of my tunnel. Also, very special thanks go to my external examiner, Dr. William A. Moses, Dean, School of Communication at Gallaudet University and to Barbara Marshall who assisted me in recruiting the informants for the study.

To other faculty members in the Department of Human Communication Studies, Dr. Richard Wright, Dr. Carolyn Stroman, Dr. David Woods, and Professor Debyii Thomas, I say thanks. I could not have succeeded without their help and support. Thanks also go to Dr. Laura Fleet, for listening, for caring, and for sharing. Also, a very special thanks is given to Dr. Orlando Taylor, Interim Vice-President for Academic Affairs at Howard University, for his support and encouragement.

To my friends Dr. Inyang Isong, Dr. Umo Isong, Dr. Armado Rodriquez, Dr. Enid Bogle, Dr. Basil Bryan, Dr. Ruth Rhone, Trevor Blake, Gladstone Christie, Joylene Griffiths-Irving, Maurice Hall, Eno Isong, Ronald Jackson, Carlos Morrison, Brenda Mveng, Michelle Mveng, Jane Norman, Gary Peade, and Diana Rowe who assisted me in ways great and small, I extend my gratitude. Special thanks go to Pamela Gordon, of St. Gabriel's Catholic School, who gave freely of her time and energy to transport my son home from school every day. That was tremendous service. Also, special thanks go to Antonio Barnes, an International Business major and Senior at Howard University, who helped me to create the diagrams in this study. To Erlinda O. Cooper CPS, of Gallaudet University, who helped me with the typing of the manuscript, I also extend thanks. I also extend thanks to the staff and students at Lister Mair Gilbey School for the Deaf, and the staff and students at Gallaudet University for helping to make this study possible.

To my parents, Mr. and Mrs. Jeremiah Davis, I extend deepest gratitude. They taught me how to cope with and triumph over adversity. For all they have given and are continuing to give, their only expectation is my happiness.

Finally, I say thanks to my son and best friend, Thomas, who laughed when I laughed, and who hugged me when I cried.

Abstract

This study asserts that Goffman's (1963) theory of stigma does not account for cultural variables which affect how deaf individuals deal with the perception that deafness is negatively different. It then posits that deaf individuals in selected cultures use different rules to contend with this perception. The study uses the metatheoretical premises of the interpretive paradigm and collects data from four focus groups of deaf individuals. It adopts Lincoln and Guba's (1985) Constant Comparison Method to qualitatively describe and compare how two groups of Jamaicans, one group of African Americans, and one group of White Americans argue with the perception of negative difference. The informants were between eighteen and twenty-two years of age, and were from educational institutions in Jamaica and the United States. The study reveals that stigma is transactional. Deaf persons locate stigma in the sender, and as they exert control over their communication interactions, they become agents in the transaction between themselves and hearing persons. Second, deaf persons who regard themselves as part of the deaf culture are proud of their cultural identity and do not defensively cower as Goffman suggests. Third, the metatheoretical assumptions of the interpretive paradigm guided the study to facilitate the emergence of another perspective on stigma from the voices of deaf persons themselves and not from a nomothetic covering law.

The study disputes Goffman's functionalist approach on the following bases: 1) an ontology of separateness does not exist between deaf and hearing persons; 2) his theory cannot always predict and control the realties of deaf individuals; 3) a discrete dualism does not exist between himself as an inquirer and the mixed contact of deaf and hearing persons as the observed, and 4) that deafness does not always cause stigma. The present study also notes that Goffman's methodology is based on case studies which functionalist researchers dismiss as "scientifically worthless."

Finally, the study makes several suggestions to the Jamaican Government, African American and White American researchers who are deaf, as well as to the Historically Black college, Howard University, to facilitate communication between the deaf and hearing cultures.

Contents

Chapter 1

Voices from the deaf cultures

White Americans:

Hearing people have no understanding of us. They don't know how we feel.

African Americans:

They want to do the thinking for you.

Jamaicans:

They have no idea what we can and cannot do.

(Excerpts from focus group interviews, Spring 1995)

Introduction and Background

Deafness as a Physiological Condition

From a physiological perspective, deafness is a condition which prevents those affected from hearing and processing all, or some of, the sound waves that reach the eardrum. This condition prompts various responses from hearing members of society. These responses include curiosity, avoidance, pity, fear, overprotection, understanding, patience, and empathy. However, each response derives from either of two dominant and competitive perspectives on deafness.

Deafness as a Culture

One perspective portrays deafness as a cultural phenomenon. Large numbers of deaf and hearing individuals support this view. Jankowski (1991) makes the distinction that "Deaf," with a capital "D", refers to members of the Deaf culture, while "deaf" with a small "d" means the person is only audiologically deaf. She advises that the Deaf culture encompasses several variables: (1) "Deaf people use sign language to communicate" (p.143); (2) "[They] ... value eye contact even more than hearing people"(p. 147); (3) "Socializing ... is highly cherished ..."(p.143); and (4) "Deaf folklore is a tradition that takes on many forms" (p.147).

This study, therefore, proposes a further distinction among persons who are audiologically deaf and culturally deaf. It speculates that individuals who regard themselves as a part of deaf culture may have common group responses to stigma. On the other hand, those who are only audiologically deaf, may engage in the de-stigmatigization process with individually selected behaviors.

Research suggests that the categorization of deaf individuals as part of a culture began in the nineteenth century, when "coming from diverse ethnic and regional backgrounds ... they fashioned a subculture with their own ... language ... associations, and their own newspapers ...." (van Cleve and Crouch, 1989 p. 169). But while the nineteenth century marks a period of cultural awareness, the scarcity of written accounts of deaf people during and shortly after the Colonial era makes it difficult to determine exactly when this awareness began.

Deafness as a Stigmatizing Condition

The second and more dominant perspective regards deafness as a disability and stigmatizing condition. "The deaf are slow to comprehend a new idea...." (McAndrew, 1948 p. 73), thus the prevalent view from hearing society is that deaf people who are ... 'disabled' ... 'have communication disorders...' " Jankowski, 1991, p. 147). Consequently, when deafness is perceived as a stigmatizing condition, negative public attitudes towards the disabled in general apply to the deaf in particular. These attitudes include avoidance and fear.

Much evidence of stigmatizing attitudes towards deafness and other types of disabilities is documented in disability research (Allport, 1958; DuBrow, 1965; Goffman, 1963; Hardaway, 1988; Katz, et al. 1978; Phillips, 1990; Sussman, 1994; Zola, 1993) which spans nearly four decades, beginning in the 1940's. Interest in disability research increased with the vast numbers of injured persons, who faced difficulties adjusting to their disabilities, during World War II. *The Journal of Social Issues* (1948) records many of these socio-psychological approaches to the study of disability, which focussed mainly on negative responses to disability. These studies are among those which informed the work of a sociologist, Erving Goffman (1963), whose theory of stigma has become a leading framework for research on the life experiences of people with physical impairments in the United States (Frank, 1988).

The basis of Goffman's approach is attribution theory which focusses on "the processes by which people come to understand their own behavior and that of others" (Littlejohn, 1992 p. 139). Goffman explains:

> When a stranger comes into our presence, then, first appearances are likely to enable us to anticipate his [sic] category and attributes, ... we ... [transform] them into normative expectations ... . (p.2)

Goffman equates stigma with an undesired "differentness" of three types which he identifies as physical deformities; "blemishes of individual character" such as homosexuality and unemployment; and stigmas of race, nationality, and religion. He argues that stigma is best explained by reference to the notion of deviation from norms and as such the stigma is a "failing, a shortcoming, a handicap" (p.3). By focussing on the perceiver who infers causes from overt behavior, Goffman's perspective assigns meanings to behavior on the basis of perception of a condition.

Criticisms Against Goffman's Theory of Stigma

However, while Goffman's work contributes significantly to disability research (Sussman, 1994), various researchers note limitations to his perspective. The present study re-groups some of these criticisms of the generalizability of Goffman's theory into four communication themes. The fifth communication theme is the focus of this study.

The first communication concern refers to the perception of stigma in intrapersonal communication. Goffman's theory does not explain how stigma operates over the course of individual lives (Glaser and Strauss, 1967). In other words, does a stigmatized condition remain a stigma during the entire life of the individual? Or can adaptation to the condition reduce the stigma?

The second concern, which closely resembles the first, focusses on the perception of stigma in interpersonal relationships. It questions what happens to stigma in intimate or long term encounters (Thompson, 1982). Is there a possibility that these encounters may not initially define the condition as stigmatizing? Or, can these encounters reduce the stigma that may have been attached to the condition initially?

The third criticism relates to nonverbal communication. It suggests that factors other than stigma can account for avoidance of individuals with a condition perceived as different (Langer et al. 1976). Research indicates that such individuals are avoided because of the novelty of the disability.

The fourth consideration relates to miscommunication. Misunderstandings, rather than stigma, also account for the strained interactions between disabled and nondisabled individuals (Makas, 1988). These misunderstandings develop when the expectations of each individual in the interaction are unclear.

The Fifth Communication Concern

This study presents the fifth communication concern, identifying its expression in the area of intercultural communication. The study notes that Goffman's theory is "specifically concerned with the issue of mixed contacts--the moments when stigmatized and normal are in the same social situation, that is, in one another's immediate physical presence, whether in a conversation-like encounter or in the mere co-presence of an unfocused gathering" (p.12).

The study searches for evidence of missing dimensions to current knowledge of stigma and deafness by investigating whether the groups of deaf individuals respond to stigma in accordance with cultural rules. Goffman's recommendations are encouraging:

> ...What remains ... [could be] re-examined for whatever is really special to it, thereby bringing analytical coherence to what is now purely historic and fortuitous unity [of stigmatizing commonalities]. Knowing... fields like race relations...one could then go on to see analytically, how they differ... . (p.147)

In addition to being members of the deaf culture, individuals also belong to other cultures including economic class, gender, and nationality.

In this study, the missing dimensions center on the deaf in ethnic cultures, economic class culture, as well as on high and low context cultures.

The Problem

This study recognizes that numerous differences which exist among individuals make it difficult to identify exactly what constitutes a culture among groups of individuals. However, "there is a middle ground where we can respectably speak of central tendencies among groups of people, a modality tendency" (Dodd, 1991 p.43). Within these cultures, there are rules or procedures prescribing expected behavior.

This study speculates that there are deaf individuals who might belong to a deaf culture and who might disregard the attribution that because they are deaf they are negatively different. The researcher speculates further that by also belonging to other cultures, these individuals who are deaf might have culturally and individually determined modes of behavior which help them to do this. The study investigates whether these behaviors are rule guided, as within cultures, or whether individuals learn a set of appropriate behaviors called roles and rules for using them (Infante et al. 1990).

The study focuses on Jamaicans who are deaf and living in Jamaica to determine their response to the perception that deafness is a negative condition, as well as to determine if their responses and behaviors are rule guided. Jamaica is selected because very little is known about individuals who are deaf in that country. The study also examines the stigma of deafness in the interethnic contexts of selected African and White American individuals who are deaf.

Jamaicans Who Are Deaf

Colonialism and the distribution of wealth in Jamaica have resulted in a gap between the rich and the poor "which represents an affront to social conscience" (Manley,1990 p. 85). These gaps have created co-cultures stratified on different levels. These levels include the owners of the means of production in the capitalist class, large farmers, the upper middle class and intelligentsia, small farmers and peasants, the lower middle class, and the working class. The cultures developed from this stratification have their own world views and attitudes which constitute group solidarity.

Not much is published about the deaf and other groups of Jamaicans who are disabled (Thorburn, 1993a). This present study presents the problem that some Jamaicans who might consider themselves part of a deaf culture also belong to one of the larger societal cultures defined by economic class. This study discusses a sample of those Jamaicans who are deaf and who also belong to a larger culture of the "average" working class. Manley (1990) describes some characteristics of the Jamaican working class:

> A communal instinct lurks in the consciousness of the average [Jamaican] .... This Jamaican displays to a remarkable degree an instinct for 'good works' [for example], ... If a Jamaican worker is suspended without pay, it is natural for his brothers on the job to rally with voluntary contributions and make up his pay. ... (p.48)

The study speculates that with this "instinct for good works," the working class as a culture might, as a rule, tend to have as part of its world view respect for traditional institutions such as family, schools and church as well as the maintenance of "good" relationships with others. To maintain such good relationships, this culture would perhaps reflect attitudes aimed at reducing and/or avoiding conflict. This group of individuals might therefore respond to stigmatizing behaviors not only from the cultural perspective of the deaf but from an awareness of the larger working class cultural rule requiring respect for traditional authority, as well as the need to maintain good relationships by reducing or avoiding conflict.

African Americans and White Americans who are Deaf

Both African Americans and White Americans who are deaf belong to larger and different ethnic groupings of African American and White Americans. Research suggests that African Americans belong to a group stigmatized on the basis of race (Higgins, 1980 p.127). As African Americans who are deaf belong to the larger African American group, this study questions whether they are also stigmatized on the basis of deafness. Hairston and Smith (1983) find that they are: "...when the conditions of Blackness and deafness are combined in one person, the individual effects of prejudice, discrimination, and negative self image are compounded exponentially" (p. ix). Thus, the present study speculates that if confronted with the double stigma of race and deafness, these individuals might choose appropriate rule guided behaviors from their ethnic grouping as well as from the deaf culture if they consider themselves to be members.

Deafness is not Inevitably Stigmatizing

> Often, to the astonishment of hearing people, Deaf people do not feel disabled. The ethnocentrism of many hearing people leads them to believe that Deaf people, upon being given a choice, would flock to seek new cures that would make them hear. ...An awareness of these stereotypes will enable hearing people to develop a better understanding of Deaf people. ... (Jankowski, 1991 pp. 147-148)

This study interprets Jankowski's assertion that "Deaf people do not feel disabled" to mean that deafness is not a disability and therefore not a stigmatizing condition. With reference to this assertion, this study speculates that stigma is transactional. For the person who is deaf to feel stigmatized, she too must also perceive deafness negatively. Further, the creation of stigma depends on the cultural rules and individual choices that the person who is deaf brings to the interpretation and formation of an alternative social reality. Although there is no research evidence of the individual choices and cultural rules employed in the following interaction, it attempts to illustrate this study's speculation that for stigma to develop both the hearing and deaf person must perceive deafness as negative.

> After watching [some] deaf people [interact], a hearing man wrote a note and handed it to one of them. The note was passed among the deaf people and finally reached him. It read, 'Can you read and write English?' The young deaf man wrote, 'No. Can you?' It was passed back to the hearing man who read it and looked dumbfounded. (Higgins, 1980, p. 134)

The need for this study arises from the perspective that behaviors are culture specific (Cronen and Shuter, 1983) and this study recognizes the need for research on cultural rules and behaviors "... in order to understand the relationship between sociocultural complexity and the status of the disabled [deaf] in both Western and non-Western societies." (Scheer and Groce, 1988 p. 27) Also, Schneider (1988) argues for "... a perspective on disability as rooted in social interaction and culture rather than in the bodies and minds of those we call 'handicapped' and 'disabled'." (p. 64)

Goffman developed his theory from a socio-psychological perspective and, in accordance with the functionalist paradigm, he probes for law-like generalizations "... true across many situations and many different time periods." (Infante, et al. 1990 p. 64) This present study proposes to investigate responses to stigma within the context of culturally determined rules as well as from the perspective of the interpretive paradigm to disclose meanings for culture and deafness. The interpretive paradigm suggests that the subjective and intersubjective experiences of people create reality. It focusses on understanding and explaining how human beings actively create cultures. The interpretive or naturalistic paradigm provides researchers with a coherent way of understanding how individuals manage their multiple realities. This paradigmatic perspective suggests that human behavior cannot be measured and, therefore, cannot be predicted and controlled. It suggests further that working hypotheses rather than generalizations should be drawn from contextual investigations and that naturalistic investigations seek to ensure "credible and dependable" data to develop from the naturally occurring discourse of informants.

This present study, therefore, proposes that the data and findings be appreciated within the context of the naturalistic paradigm and not from the functionalist perspective which seeks to derive universal and generalizable laws from research. This study proposes that unless stigma is studied from a communication perspective, nomothetic sociological and psychological analyses will be inappropriately applied to this communication phenomenon.

Significance of the Study

It is hoped that an awareness of the differences of the impact of culture on how persons who are deaf view themselves and others who view them as negatively different will help legislators, educators, care givers and others who interact with the deaf culture in Jamaica and the United States to avoid stereo-typical categorizations of these groups. Hairston and Smith (1983) caution: "Generalizing or stereotyping about [the deaf culture] can present many barriers to helping individual members, particularly with respect to the planning of educational programs and the effective use of such support services as rehabilitation and guidance." (p. 2)

With specific reference to Jamaica, the study speculates that as the Jamaican Government is currently soliciting information from interest groups for its proposed legislation on persons with disabilities, the findings of this study may: 1) serve as reference for the deaf as a specific group; 2) identify ways in which the hearing culture may facilitate more effective communication with the deaf culture; 3) provide information in international fora on deafness in Jamaica and the Caribbean region; and 4) stimulate further research on deafness in Jamaica and the Caribbean. Because of the lack of information on deafness in Jamaica, the 1994 International Conference on deafness concluded its discussions without reference to the deaf culture in Jamaica or in the

Caribbean basin (Erting et al. 1994).

Research Questions and Definitions

Two research questions guide this study:

1. **What links, if any, can be demonstrated among culture, deafness, and stigma?**

This study searches for possible links among these three variables. Culture includes the habits, practices, meanings, perceptions, and conventions of a group of people; their language and other communicative tools not only develop from these habits, practices and perceptions, but dialectically influence and re-shape these variables that gave rise to them. Stigma is discussed as a convergence of negative perceptions rooted in culture and communicated to members of that culture. Therefore, as members of the deaf culture regard deafness as a cultural phenomenon, the study seeks to find out how this cultural perception of deafness affects responses to stigma.

2. **What constitutive or regulative rules may be derived for selected deaf populations for dealing with stigmatization?**

The present study recognizes Goffman's invaluable contribution to the study of stigma but seeks to determine whether the deaf culture uses constitutive and/or regulative rules to deal with the perception of some hearing persons that deafness is negatively different. To conduct its investigation, the study is guided by the theory of Coordinated Management of Meaning (CMM) (Pearce & Cronen, 1980) which views people as acting on the basis of constitutive rules (rules of meaning) and regulative rules (rules of action) to understand and interpret the events they experience. CMM suggests that human communication is inherently imperfect and that "people can have perfectly satisfactory co-ordination without understanding each other [as they] organize their actions in ways that seem logical to all parties...[even though] they understand [each other]...in a variety of different ways" (Littlejohn, 1995, p. 207). This present study questions whether each cultural group utilizes different rules as well as makes individual choices in how they respond to stigma. To investigate whether or not they make individual choices, the study is guided by the concept of Personal Communication World View which assumes "that individuals adopt from their cultures, and from their personalities, a system of thinking about the amount of control, influence, choice, and regulation they can exert in their communication climates" (Dodd, 1991 p. 83). In using cultural rules and making personal choices, individuals who are deaf might express different attitudes and behaviors towards stigma. These may range on a continuum from acceptance to rejection.

Stigma Defined

This study discusses stigma as a transactional phenomenon. It defines stigma as the communication of converged cultural perceptions of two or more individuals or groups that a condition unique to one individual or group is negative. Both the observer and bearer of the condition must, therefore, perceive the condition as negatively different. However, Goffman (1963) advises that the Greeks originated the term **stigma** to refer to bodily signs designed to expose something unusual and bad about the moral status of the signifier. He notes that they (the Greeks) cut or burnt signs into the bodies of slaves, criminals and traitors to indicate that these persons should be avoided, especially in public places.

> Later, in Christian times, two layers of metaphors were added to the term: the first referred to bodily signs of holy grace that took the form of eruptive blossoms on the skin; the second, a medical allusion to this religious allusion, referred to bodily signs of physical disorder. (p.2)

Culture Defined

Despite extensive usage, the term 'culture' is not easily defined. In a study seeking to identify a definition of the term, Kroeber and Kluckhohn (1952) uncovered 164 definitions (Klopf, 1987 p. 26) each of which identify important aspects of culture. For example, Murdock (1956) describes culture as tendencies and habits defining behavior, and not the behavior itself, while Dodd (1991) relates culture to a kaleidoscope with similar shapes but different colors, or with different shapes but similar colors.

The present study defines culture as groups of individuals sharing similar meanings, norms, beliefs and behaviors which allow such individuals to share a common world view. Within each society there are different cultures and when these cultures interact, the process is described as intercultural communication. In this interaction, cultures may be identified on the basis of whether they are "in-groups," those with whom members of other cultures identify, or "out-groups," those with whom other members of other cultures do not identify. This study speculates that in-group and out-group communication might affect the relationship between African American and White American individuals who are deaf as well as their attitudes towards stigma. This is possible within a framework of interrethnic communication characterized by "suspicion ... stereotyping ... [and] solidarity" (Dodd, 1991 pp. 109-110).

Cultural Rules Defined

The present study defines cultural rules as expected and common behaviors in response to specific stimuli. To support this definition, the study refers to Shimanoff's (1980) theory which discusses a rule as a "followable prescription that indicates what behavior is obligated, preferred, or prohibited in certain contexts" (p.24). This study makes specific reference to constitutive and regulative rules discussed in the theory of Coordinated Management of Meaning as rules which help individuals to understand and interpret their experiences. "Constitutive rules are essentially rules of meaning, used by communicators to interpret or understand an event. Regulative rules are essentially rules of action, used to determine how to respond or behave" (Littlejohn, 1992 p. 203).

Organization of the Study

This research effort is divided into six chapters. Chapter one contains the general introduction to the entire study. Chapter two provides the literature review. Chapter three discusses the theoretical framework. Chapter four discusses the research design and methodology. Chapter five contains the research findings of interviews with the selected deaf cultures and Chapter six presents the discussions, implications, limitations, and recommendations for future research.

Chapter 2

Literature Review

As stigmatizing attitudes towards disability in general relate to deafness specifically (Higgins, 1980), the literature reviewed on stigmatization of persons with disabilities also relates to persons who are deaf. The literature review discusses: 1) disability as a stigmatizing condition from 1948, when much of the result of early disability research was published, to 1994; 2) the deaf culture of the three selected groups; and 3) cultural responses to disability.

Early Research

Negative attitudes towards persons with disabilities span millennia:

> The Lord said unto Moses, "Say to Aaron: for the generations to come, none of your descendants who has a defect may come near to offer the food of his God. No man who has any defect may come near; no man with a crippled foot or hand, or who is hunchbacked, or dwarfed, or who has any eye defect, or who has festering or running sores or damaged testicles." ... (Leviticus, Chapter 21: verses 16 to 23)

In another reference, a character, Homer, describes another character, Thersites, as "the ugliest man in the camp, squinting, lame on one foot, hunchbacked, with a deformed skull and sparse hair" (Illiad 11, 216-219 quoted in von Hentig, 1948). While the Greeks negatively imply that a crooked mind is in a crooked body, Williams (1918) titles his novel *The Man With the Clubfoot* and seems to be presenting disability as folkloric trivia.

While disability has long been regarded as negative, social psychologists were among the early researchers to investigate disability and its effects. Much of the result of early research work was published in the 1948 disability issue of the *Journal of Social Issues*. Barker (1948), who initiated the proposal for the publication, is one of the first researchers to identify disability as stigmatizing: "No amount of optimistic talk can remove the fact that, other things being equal, a physically disabled person is relatively ineffective in a social world devised for physically normal persons" (p. 35). Some of his colleagues concur: "There are many factors within the individual and within the society in which he [sic] lives that render him [sic] incapable of dealing with his disability..." (Cutsforth, 1948 p. 62). "In many cases, the child [with a disability] becomes a social isolate..." (Cain, 1948 p. 92). "Today,... the disabled ...carry the sign ... Help Wanted" (Rusk and Taylor, 1948, p. 101).

However, Meyerson (1988) criticizes disability research in this period as "meager, trivial and molecular... So many conclusions are stated in terms of common stereotypes...[There is a] lack of guiding theory to indicate meaningful questions clearly, and define them precisely" (p. 182-183). For example, while Barker's (1948) thesis describes persons with disabilities as relatively ineffective, he admits that such "explanations suffer ... from the absence of data ... and [are] primitive concepts lacking conceptual and operational clarity" (p. 29).

Identifying these research weaknesses, other researchers disagree that disability is generally stigmatizing. Ladieu (et al. 1948) criticize Barker's findings:

> Neither the injured, nor the non-injured could expect, for example, to have a leg amputee play on a company baseball team which competes with other teams. The injured man might **miss** the activity keenly, but knowing that he cannot meet the physical requirements, he is not apt to see the situation as one of non-acceptance. Non-acceptance, from his point of view, is a one sided affair, resting primarily on the negative attitudes of the non-injured. ...the margin of difference between the two points of view may spell the difference between non-participation and non-acceptance of the injured person. ... If however, the difference is resolved, the situation merely becomes an instance of non-participation, and the problem of acceptance does not arise. (pp. 56-57)

According to Meyerson (1948a), undesirable behavior reported for persons with physical disabilities arises because these persons have been subjected to different kinds of life experiences. She argues that the literature does not indicate a one-to-one relationship between disability and behavior and that:

> The key problems are ... to create concepts that will enable us to order and understand what is found. When it is possible to do this, it will also be possible to explain why and how certain physical characteristics may result in one person developing psychological encystment, a second becoming aggressive, and a third showing no apparent defects. (p. 68)

In another study, Cruickshank (1948) approaches the problem of adjustment from a phenomenological perspective and discovers that in social relationships the individual with a disability attempts to insure not her physical organic self but her phenomenal self, the concept of herself of which she is cognizant. As a result, he contends that:

> ...the adjustive problems of the handicapped child in the home and community are no different from those of the normal child except (1) in instances where the handicap itself is organically irremovable, (2) when the handicap cannot be compensated for by the child, or (3) when the handicap functionally stands for something irreparable to the child. (p. 78)

Cruickshank suggests that the child with a disability faces not only the normal problems of self expansion and maintenance of self-concept but the adjustive problems which result exclusively from the physical handicap. He contends that the failure to recognize the duality of the problem accounts for much of the misunderstanding with reference to persons who are disabled. Cruickshank's analysis is based on Lowman and Seidenfeld (1947) study of the effects of poliomyelitis on the social adjustments of 437 persons.

A Minority Status for the Disabled

The decade of the fifties begins with a report commissioned by the Social Science Research Council from researchers Barker, Wright, Meyerson and Gonick (1953). They identify some parallels between the stigmatizing conditions of people with disability and the situations of deprived minority groups. This minority status of "the disabled" became an "intuitively and experientially appealing concept that gained rapid assent ... [offering] a radically new and different way of defining, thinking about, and remedying ... a social-psychological problem" (Meyerson, p. 175).

During this period, some researchers suggest that positive relationships between persons with and without disability can develop (Homans, 1950; Allport, 1958). However, other researchers continue to emphasize stigmatizing effects of disability. Granofsky (1955) finds that a short period of contact between persons with and without disability (approximately eight hours) does not alter negative attitudes towards the former group, while Force (1956) indicates significant differences between both groups comprising children in status scores as friends, playmates and workmates.

Suggesting that individuals with disabilities need to be combative, Tenny (1953) argues that they should confront the belief of individuals without disability that they are second class citizens, but Allport (1958) counters that the human mind must think with the aid of categories. "... Most of the business of life can go on with less effort if we stick together with our own kind ... It is not that we have class prejudice, but only that we find comfort and ease in our own..." (p. 18).

By 1960, the Miami Conference on Research in the Psychological Aspects of Rehabilitation concludes that, in interacting with persons with disabilities, a person without disabilities is not likely to be sure what kind of behavior is expected and appropriate and fears unintentionally hurting the former's feelings. This uneasiness also results from the fact that the person without disabilities has not been able to learn to feel at ease and how to behave toward those with disabilities (Kelly et al. 1960). The literature also suggests that even some medical professionals stigmatize persons with disabilities. Solnit and Stark, (1961) recall a physician's comment to the mother of a child who was disabled: "You might as well put her in an institution and let her die in peace" (p. 530). On the other hand, Plank and Horwood (1961) report the instance of medical personnel who took the time to understand a child's behavior after her leg was amputated and were able to help her develop positive and trusting relationships with a large number of people.

Davis (1961) marks a departure from traditional research methodological approaches. He interviewed a number of persons who are disabled to find out how they handle the imputation that they are not normal like everyone else. One interviewee remarks: "I get suspicious when somebody says 'Let's go for a uh, ah [imitates confused and halting speech] push with me down the hall,' or something like that ... they're aware, really aware, that there's a wheelchair here, and that this is probably uppermost with them..." (p. 123). And another, who was visiting a friend reports that a woman whom she had never met before, walked right up to her: Gee, what do you have? How long have you been that way? Oh gee, that's terrible!' "And so I answered her questions, but I got very annoyed and wanted to say, 'Lady, mind your own business' " (p.

127). Davis argues that the interactional problems of persons with visible disabilities are not so dissimilar from those that confront individuals without disabilities. "If only now and then, and to a lesser degree, we too on occasions find ourselves in situations in which some uncamouflageable attribute of ours jars the activity and the expectations of our company" (p. 132).

In 1963, Goffman published "Stigma: Notes on the Management of Spoiled Identity" in which he defines the term "stigma" and outlines its implications for individuals with disabilities in the United States of America.

> ...while the stranger is present before us, evidence can arise of his possessing an attribute that makes him different from others. ...He is thus reduced in our minds from a whole and usual person, to a tainted, discounted one. Such an attribute is a stigma, especially when its discrediting effect is very extensive... it is...a failing, a shortcoming, a handicap. (p. 3)

Goffman argues that stigma is best explained by reference to the notion of deviation from norms and that a person is not a deviant until his acts or attributes are perceived as negatively different. He also suggests that it is not the functional limitations of impairment which constitute the greatest problems faced by persons with disabilities but rather societal and social responses to disability. He advises that his analysis is limited to "moments when stigmatized and normal are in the same social situation, that is, in one another's immediate presence..." (p. 12), but comments on the management of group stigma:

> A good portion of those who fall within a given stigma category [for example deafness] may well refer to the total membership by the term 'group' or an equivalent, such as [culture] 'we,' or 'our people,' ... however,...they will neither have the capacity for collective action nor a stable and embracing pattern of mutual interaction.... . (p.23)

Goffman's thesis therefore seems to condemn individuals who are deaf to inevitable stigmatization.

Sussman (1994) acknowledges that it is Goffman's work, more than any other, that researchers cite as exemplifying the application of deviance theory to the study of disability. Although Goffman's treatise contributes significantly to disability research, many of the early 1948 studies, flawed by theoretical weakness, provide the foundation for his work, a fact which Goffman himself recognizes. He credits several researchers for "having done good work on stigma" (p. 1).

However some researchers recognize limitations to Goffman's treatise.

"Goffman's (1963) theory of stigma presupposes a dichotomy between 'us' and 'them' in situations in which stigma arises. ...[and] keeps the focus upon the strained interactions between the disabled and 'normals' (Frank, 1988, p. 106). Glaser and Strauss (1967) argue that Goffman's description of the effects of stigma, in isolated instances, obviates systematic understanding of how stigma operates over the course of individual lives. In addition, they contend that his theory does not emphasize exceptions or differences in attitudes relating to stigma.

Gaier et al. (1967) are not convinced of the stigmatizing effects of relationships between persons with and without disabilities, arguing that evidence on the attitudinal effects of personal contact with those who differ psychologically and physically remains anonymous. Langer et al. (1976) advise that individuals who are not disabled may avoid those with a disability not because of stigma, but because disability is a novel stimulus. Langer and his colleagues advance their novel stimulus hypothesis, explaining that, while verbal and nonverbal expressions of affect may correlate highly, nonverbal indices of negativity may simply reflect discomfort and conflict without concomitant derogation. They advise that conceptualizing persons with disabilities as novel stimuli instead of stigmatized individuals could get them accepted by individuals who are not disabled. One way to do that, they suggest, is to explain to persons who are disabled that being stared at does not necessarily imply unfavorable attitudes.

Thompson (1982) also challenges Goffman's theory, claiming that it does not account for what happens to stigma over time and in intimate or long term encounters. In another study, Murphy et al. (1988) also depart from Goffman's thesis, proposing their liminality model, in which they view persons who are disabled as having an undefined status, neither being ill nor well, neither socially alive nor socially expunged and removed. This hypothesis results from a three year anthropological investigation of the social relations of paraplegics and quadriplegics in the New York metropolitan area. Murphy and his colleagues concentrate on people living in the community, outside of the hospital setting, and find that these persons with disabilities "dwell in a kind of limbo" in their interactions with others. Makas (1988) concludes that the strain that frequently occurs during interactions between persons who are disabled and those who are not disabled may derive more from misunderstandings of one another's expectations than from negative intentions.

Other scholars recognize that Goffman's treatise does not fully account for changes in the political/social situation which empower individuals who are disabled in the de-stigmatization process. For example, Hahn (1985) recognizes definitional shifts in the study of disability which indicate that disability [and consequently stigma] is the product of the interaction between the individual and the environment. According to Hahn, this socio-political definition of disability implies that:

> Disability stems from the failure of a structured social environment to adjust to the needs and aspirations of disabled citizens rather than from the inability of a disabled individual to adapt to the demands of society. In viewing disability as a product of a dynamic interaction between humans and their surroundings, emphasis is shifted from the individual to the broader social, cultural, economic, and political environment.... (p. 93)

Also, Scotch (1988) recognizes the role of politics and the social structure in defining issues, adding that the United States government contributes to the redefinition of disability. Specifically he mentions Section 504 of the Rehabilitation Act of 1973 and the Education for all Handicapped Children Act of 1975. He notes:

> The programmatic effects of these statutes ... dramatically [increased] the accessibility of public education, employment, government services, and public facilities to disabled people. Of equal or greater importance, however, were the definitions included in the new laws, which focussed on a broad group of people in a way that aided the formation of a social movement. (p. 167)

Discussing stigma from a political perspective, Anspach (1979) disagrees with Goffman's suggestion that persons with disabilities are stigmatized captive, and argues that, to the contrary, they are politically active. He develops a typology of four modal responses to stigma, which individuals with disabilities utilize in interaction with those who are not. Referencing the work of previous researchers, Anspach identifies these stratagems as normalization (Davis, 1975), disassociation (Davis, 1972), and political activism. He contends that political activism creates an ideology that repudiates societal values and normative standards, and gives rise to a viable self-conception for participants.

Support for Goffman

In spite of the limitations identified, Exline & Winters (1965) and Kleck et al. (1966) are among researchers who utilize and confirm Goffman's deviance model of impairment. Novak and Lerner (1968) argue that individuals who are not disabled avoid those who are, believing that the impairment could also happen to them. As well, Thompson (1981) examines interpersonal skills of stigmatized and nonstigmatized children and finds that the stigmatized children become deficient communicators as a result of their social isolation. Support for Goffman's hypothesis continues in the nineties with Ablon (1990) arguing that, in the case of dwarfism, "a physical difference also carries with it historical and cultural baggage that has created a mythic stereotype. ... Much of the ambivalence and problematic behavior exhibited...is caused by a confusion generated by having to reconcile realistic similarities and differences, mythic stereotypes and cultural images" (p. 885). Hardaway (1990) sums up the attitudes of persons without disabilities towards those who are as "pathological." In defending Goffman's thesis, Sussman (1994) contends that the sociologist does not view the link between stigma/deviance and disability as inevitable. She contends that Goffman does not claim that people with disabilities are inevitably passive and victimized. Instead, Goffman holds that the meaning of disability is social and changeable. Researchers (Hahn, 1985 and Scotch, 1988) support this assertion, documenting evidence that people actively create their own reality.

While Goffman's thesis gained popularity in the sixties, Kohlberg (1969) discussed cognitive development as another perspective on stigma. This theory emphasizes stigmatizing reactions evolving in predictable stages. "[Stigma might be linked] to growing capacities to discriminate among people, categorize them into groups, form one's identity in relation to others. If this is correct, stigmatizing reactions might evolve through predictable stages" (Ainlay et al. 1986, p.190).

During this period, the literature reviewed also suggests that the once hard-and-fast distinction between social deviance and political marginality was becoming blurred. "An ever-increasing array of personal habits, from long hair to the discarding of brassieres, to vegetarianism, came to be equated with conscious rebellion against the confines of the normative order" (Horowitz and Liebowitz 1968 p. 765). "...Increasing numbers of disabled people embraced political activism and political action and demanded integration into the mainstream of American society ... [Among them were] blind ... deaf ... and disabled war veterans" (Scotch, 1988 p. 160). Thus the sixties saw the beginnings of political activism among individuals with disabilities and other stigmatized groups.

A New Beginning

By the 1970s, organizations had been formed that encompassed individuals with a wide range of physical disabilities (Scotch, 1988). In 1974, the President's Committee on the Employment of the Handicapped (PCEH) became the first national coalition of activists with disabilities when it organized itself as the American Coalition of Citizens with Disabilities (ACCD). This organization linked several local and single-disability organizations and, according to Scotch, the ACCD was to become a major advocate for incorporating civil rights guarantees for people with disabilities into federal laws and regulations. Other organizations of people with disabilities including the Disabled in Action, National Center for Law, Handicapped in South Bend, Disability Rights Center, the National Association for the Deaf, Paralyzed Veterans of America, and the American Council of the Blind developed and mushroomed during this period.

By 1977, about 300 persons with disabilities went to United States Department of Health, Education and Welfare, carrying placards, shouting slogans and chanting songs from the civil rights movement. This movement coincided with other demonstrations of individuals with disabilities in other major cities, and they were all protesting Secretary Califano's failure to sign Section 504 of the Rehabilitation Act, which forbids architectural and economic discrimination on the basis of disability (Anspach, 1979). The Bill was subsequently signed. "Increasingly, ...the federal government considered and enacted policies prohibiting discrimination on the basis of disability. ...Positions on issues were debated... agreements reached...a viable movement had been constructed..." (Scotch, 1988, p. 166).

During this period, new concepts in the literature on disability began to emerge. **Deinstitutionalization** "forbids any [disabled] person to be admitted to the institution unless prior determination shall have been made that residence in the institution is the least restrictive habilitation setting" (Wyatt v. Stickney, 3195 U.S. 3 1972); "...**normalization** [allows] mentally retarded people...conditions of everyday living...as close as possible to...society..." (Nirje, 1976 p. 231); and "**mainstreaming**...[integrates] disabled children into regular educational programs whenever possible..." (DeWeaver, 1983 p. 435). But Rubin and Peplau (1975) caution that social injustice may still be perpetuated because there is a tendency to perceive others as deserving their fates.

New theoretical perspectives on stigma also began to develop at this time. The psychoanalytic approach views stigma as emotionally contextual, primarily related to emotional conflicts arising from a child's biological urges and early experiences with parents (Ashmore and Del Boca, 1976), while Social Learning Theory (Bandura, 1977) discusses "[stigma] as sets of learned behaviors that develop through the interaction among the modeled behaviors to which the child is exposed, the expectancy of reinforcement for those behaviors, and the current physical/cognitive skill level of the child. ...[Therefore], our social environment is critical in determining whether or not we stigmatize, whom we stigmatize, and how we stigmatize" (Ainlay et al.1986, p.189). This present study recognizes that the converse is also true and suggests that not only the social but the cultural environment determine whether or not individuals who are deaf feel stigmatized, who stigmatizes them, and how they respond to such stigmatizing behaviors.

Bynder and New (1976) caution that, although researchers are now working within broader frameworks, their concepts are still limited and this prevents them from viewing and making statements regarding the broader consequences of disabilities. In addition, Anspach (1979) urges that the sociology of deviance should revise its conceptions to account for active attempts on the part of those labeled as deviant to mold their own identities. He emphasizes that persons with disabilities use political activism as an ideology to not only repudiate normative standards but create a viable self-conception.

Disability research in the eighties sought to classify the political movement of stigmatized groups as ideological. Kitsuse (1980) argues, that although political activism is important, the interactionist conception of the social and moral situation of deviants needs to be examined in order to identify some theoretical issues. The literature suggests that Americans are tossed about on conflicting currents of ideology, values and fundamental themes, and that new ways of thinking are emerging. One such new way of thinking is the United Nations' call for a World Program of Action for Disabled People, designating January 1, 1983 to December 31, 1992, as the Decade of Disabled Persons. The United Nations highlights equality of opportunities for the individuals with disabilities in several spheres including education, employment, biomedical research and cultural activities. In another instance, a student protest shut down Gallaudet University in the United States from March 6 to 13, 1988. Gannon 1989 reports:

> For the first time, knowledge of sign language and an understanding of deaf culture became important issues in the process of hiring a top administrator. The success of the week's protest sent a surge of elation through deaf people and their friends; it gave many a new self-image and renewed their pride in American Sign Language, deaf culture and deaf history. (p. 15)

Hahn (1985) agrees that significant changes are taking place in the stigmatizing condition of individuals with disabilities, but that research has neglected to focus sufficiently on the 'minority group perspective' of persons with disabilities. He suggests that researchers could examine aesthetic anxiety in discrimination as one basis for constitutional challenges to the unequal treatment of minorities with disabilities. However, while there is a movement for a minority status of those with disabilities, Scotch (1988) says that many people with disabilities do not identify themselves as being disabled or choose not to be part of a politically active community of persons with disabilities. And McNeil (1983) advises that, although 1 in 11 Americans of working age identify themselves as having a disability, for most of them, such identification does not translate into group consciousness or political action.

Phillips (1985) cautions that persons with disabilities seem to be confused by the meaning of success: "Does success mean the pursuit of normalization, or even the illusion of normality...or becoming an individual known primarily by...her disability? At what point can the disabled person shed the social stereotypes and be accepted as an individual who is also physiologically different?" (p. 45). Phillips suggests that the rehabilitation model of the disability rights movement continues to focus on the victim status and problems of persons with disabilities as stigmatized persons rather than assisting them in redefining criteria by which normality and success are measured.

The literature reviewed in the mid-1980s supports Scotch's observation, suggesting that in spite of the extensive political organization and activities of persons with disabilities, not much has changed in their stigmatizing condition. Pearson (1984) argues that, while quadriplegics have been allowed to die or kill themselves within the last year or two in West Virginia, the severely physically disabled are still often consigned to nursing homes. But Zola (1985) explains that there are objective differences between the disability rights movement and other minority group movements. For instance, with the increase in ethnic pride, it became possible to reclaim one's ancestry. " 'I'm proud to be Greek, Polish, or Jewish.' With the civil rights movement came 'Black is Beautiful.' With Gay liberation came 'Gay is good.' However, few disability rights leaders have proclaimed 'Thank God, I have Multiple Sclerosis,' or 'Up with Polio' " (p. 7). Zola states that in the purposeful activities of the media disability is metaphorically represented in themes including pity, fear, loathing, innocence and wonderment. As a result, the disability becomes nothing more than some barrier to be overcome in the individual's re-entry into the American way of life. Sagatun (1985) finds that social interaction between persons with and without disabilities continues to be awkward and difficult, and often, a physical handicap becomes a social handicap.

However, Murphy and his colleagues (1988) view persons with disabilities as being "caught and fixated in a passage through life that has left them socially ambivalent and ill-defined, condemned to a kind of seclusion..." (p. 235).

With research emphasis still on the stigmatizing effects of disability, scholars (Frank,1988; Makas, 1988; Mest, 1988; Schneider and Conrad 1980; and Schneider 1988) attempt to provide the literature with the perspective of individuals with disability in this period. One informant remarks, "... I have to trust somebody a lot before I tell them [about my condition], all my friends know, but in terms of my work, forget it. This is a risk I can't take ..." (Schneider and Conrad, 1980, p. 38). But, in spite of these representations, several concerns remain in the literature. Schroedel (1984) stresses that definitions of disability are problematic in all types of surveys; that given the "dynamic" nature of disability, longitudinal studies should be considered as being best able to facilitate an understanding of the phenomenon (Pope, 1984). Fine and Asch (1988) contend that the number of investigations that are flawed from inception by prejudicial common sense assumptions, theoretical bias, and methodological error remains high; and Mest (1988) concludes that the continued lack of recognition and respect for the social needs and support of people with disabilities is an important issue that must be addressed.

However, Meyerson (1988) recognizes disability research advances. "For the first time in history, people with many different kinds of disabilities, their parents, friends -- including some social science professionals --organizations, and sensitized legislators [have] joined to demand, 'Change the system' " (p. 185). Meyerson suggests that the hypothesis in part is "better attitudes follow better behavior" and, although the struggle continues, the data so far are encouraging. This study agrees with Meyerson's observations but argues that, with some researchers uncritically utilizing Goffman's theory of stigma for more than a quarter of a century, the conclusion of early disability research that disability is inevitably stigmatizing continues to characterize the literature.

> There can be no argument that Goffman and others indeed were pioneers in introducing the concepts of deviance and stigma ...However, we wonder if the followers are now relying on those few concepts a little too much as 'crutches' to explain disability. Thus whenever findings are reported, and not much more can be made of their significances, we immediately turn to Goffman and others to write a few more paragraphs. (Bynder and New, 1976 p. 45)

In 1990, the American Disabilities Act (ADA) was passed, making it "unlawful to discriminate in employment against a qualified individual with a disability...[and outlawing] discrimination against individuals with disabilities in state and local government services, public accommodations, transportation and telecommunications..." (Introductory page - unnumbered). But, "[a] law cannot guarantee what a culture cannot give" comments the *Disability Rag*, (1993). "...Yes, we have a law. But there is not a glimmer of public understanding as to what that law is supposed to mean ... [according to the Decaux Company] disabled militants are ruining the toilet projects for everyone with their stupid ADA" (p. 25).

In spite of the ADA's thrust to reduce stigmatization, the data in the decade of the nineties continue to indicate negative attitudes towards persons with disabilities. Ablon (1990) records, for example, a mother's reaction when told of her child's dwarfism:

> The physical therapist was working with him, and I asked the old question, "Why do you think his arms and legs are so short?" And she said, "Oh well, it's dwarfism," and she went on about his being a dwarf. She didn't see my reaction was just to fall backwards, because to me dwarfism or being a dwarf was the troll under the bridge in "Three Billygoats Gruff." Not **my** child! (p. 880)

The literature also reports individuals with disabilities struggling for appropriateness of labels. Hardaway (1990) argues that labels such as "handicapped" and "disabled" impose limitations, promote a negative mental picture and assure control and superiority over that particular group of people. "Thus the growing popularity of terms like TAB's and MAB's (temporarily or momentarily able bodied) to describe the general population breaks down the separateness of 'us' and 'them' and emphasizes the continuity and inevitability of 'the disability experience' (Zola, 1993 p.171). In another study, (Mwaria, 1990) recommends that persons with severe brain injuries be de-classified as stigmatized and deviant and instead be re-considered as liminal. She contends that such patients in coma do not merely violate the moral order, but that they test it, in that their very presence raises moral questions for which there are no cultural guidelines.

Finally, Sussman (1994) summarizes the literature relating to disability, stigma and deviance in the United States and contends that "the state of knowledge about the relationship between disability, on the one hand, and stigma and deviance on the other, is likely to seem a bit murky" (p. 15). She argues that while social scientists describe a variety of meanings for disability, they are not at odds with one another. Rather, each researcher contributes to the illumination of a social field on which the meaning of disability is continuously constructed (p. 21).

The Deaf as a Stigmatized Group

Higgins (1980) agrees that what has been said of persons with disability in general can be said of the deaf in particular but highlights the following five issues as characterizing stigmatizing attitudes towards individuals who are deaf:

1. The discredited deaf: He contends that, because people who are deaf look "normal", they often blend into the hearing world until their signing makes them visible and discredited: "...the animated facial, hand and body movements of the deaf sometimes alarm the hearing...[and the resulting]...quiet curiosity and stares of the hearing are interpreted by the deaf as indications of stigmatization..." (pp. 127-131).

2. Master Status: He posits that deafness becomes the master status for those outside of the hearing world: "...the individual characteristics are overlooked, while the 'failing' is emphasized...[and] not only does the larger social world emphasize the 'failing' of the outsiders, but it also treats those with the same 'failing' as if they were the same" (p. 131). Higgins emphasizes this point with the experience of a young man who was deaf and who was a student at a hearing university:

> He [the student who was deaf] asked a hearing student in a nearby dorm room to make a telephone call for him. After talking with the deaf student for a short time, the hearing student remarked that he thought all deaf people had limited interests like the deaf student's deaf roommate who sometimes showed to hearing students football cards that are included in packages of bubble gum. (p. 133)

3. Spread: Higgins advises that people who are hearing attribute other negative characteristics and limitations to the original 'failing' of deafness, generalizing that individuals who are deaf are both 'deaf and dumb,' suffering from deficient mental abilities.

4. Sizing up the outsider: He argues that because persons who are deaf are not "normal" they are "inspected to see if they measure up to the task." He recalls a man who was deaf giving the following account of what happened thirty five years ago when his fiancee who was hearing told her family that they were to be married:

Her mother hit the roof, and came down on the next train, and [I] had to go in hiding because she was so angry about it. She didn't accept the situation until it had been agreed for me to talk with the elders of the family.... . (p.137)

5. Acceptance: Higgins contends that unlike Blacks, Native Americans, gays, and many other stigmatized groups, the stigma of deafness is also a "very real physical impairment" (p. 140). He says that when communicating with persons who are hearing, individuals who are deaf are concerned with one specific issue: the willingness or reluctance of persons who are hearing to repeat their spoken message. Higgins notes that individuals who are deaf define this issue as involving social acceptance. "Repeating a spoken message is a sign of willingness to deaf people to accept them for what they are -- people with a hearing impairment who may happen to need the hearing's words repeated, no more and no less. Refusal or unwillingness to repeat a spoken message is taken by the deaf as an indication that the hearing person does not want to bother with them" (p. 141).

Higgins concludes that encounters between persons with and without disabilities are often strained, awkward, and confusing--typically impersonal and full of tension. "Unlike many other outsiders' 'failings,' deafness does inhibit interaction with the larger social world, regardless of whether the deaf are stigmatized or not" (p. 143).

African Americans and White Americans Who are Deaf

Both groups belong to larger ethnic groupings whose relationship has historically been characterized by conflict which has led to numerous disturbances and legislation to reduce the conflict. Hairston and Smith (1983) advise that the conflict between both African Americans and White Americans has affected the relationship of those individuals who are deaf. They agree that there is a racial aspect to deafness, which, to be dismissed, "would be naive and presumptuous... A Black [African American] deaf person is already at a disadvantage from the time he [she] is born. It can't be explained away and it won't go away easily. Attitudes die hard" (p. 3). Consequently, "being both Black and Deaf is [perceived] in many ways a "double whammy" because of society's abrogation of each of these two minorities" (Vernon, 1983 p. ix).

The April 1972 4th Biennial Conference of Professional Rehabilitation Workers with the Adult Deaf provides some examples of this perceived "double whammy."

1. Unemployment rates for African Americans who are deaf are much

higher than for White Americans who are deaf.

2. Very few African Americans who are deaf go beyond the eighth grade in school.

3. African Americans who are deaf, as well as their parents, are often not aware of the facilities or services that are available to them. Information on continuing education, scholarships, or training programs bypasses them.

4. Because there are so few African Americans who are deaf and professional in the field of education and rehabilitation, most African American children who are deaf have no model to emulate and are given no inspiration to succeed. (p. 1)

As "members of the Black deaf community face a struggle not shared by the deaf [culture] at large" (McCaskill-Emerson, 1992 p. 4), this present study speculates that, by belonging to the African American culture, African Americans who are deaf may have a wider range of stigmatizers who include not only hearing persons generally, but some White Americans who are deaf. Higgins (1980) supports the study's assertion with the following example:

A well-known social club for the deaf in Chicago only recently changed its policy to permit blacks to become members [but afterwards] the club moved from downtown to the north side of the city. ...Important to some white deaf was that too many black deaf ... were coming into the club. ...Since the club has been moved, fewer blacks are coming, which meets with the approval of many white deaf. (p.51)

This present study contends that unlike African Americans who are deaf, White Americans who are deaf might face less stigmatizing attitudes as they are perhaps able to confront stigmatizing attitudes on the basis of the ethnicity of the stigmatizer.

African American and White American Deaf as Belonging to a Low Context Culture

Both African Americans and White Americans who are deaf might also belong to the low context culture of the United States of America and might share similar strategies of interpreting messages. Hall (1966) notes that roles and rules differ from culture to culture, and these differences are more apparent depending on whether the culture is high or low context.

Explicit and verbal messages are emphasized in low context cultures while in high context cultures information is normally encoded in the physical context which is used to determine what is meant rather than what is said. This present study speculates that, based on the definition of low context cultures, African Americans and White Americans who are deaf might generally understand stigma by focussing on and interpreting specific actions and messages as stigmatizing or not. Reactions are then specific to such actions. The following example seeks to illustrate the point:

> ... two [deaf] friends were dining in a restaurant. One of the deaf friends was well educated, with advanced degrees. They were signing to one another, and the waitress made fun of them by mimicking their signs and gestures. At the end of the meal, the well educated deaf woman wrote a note to the waitress which explained in very sophisticated words that her behavior was rude. The waitress did not understand the note, and therefore some customers explained to her what it meant. The cashier was embarrassed by the incident and insisted that the deaf people not pay for their meals. (Higgins, 1980 p. 128)

The researcher contrasts how an individual from a high context culture might have interpreted the waitress's behavior. This is to provide further insight as to how messages are interpreted in a low context culture. From a high context perspective, an individual who is deaf might not have determined that the behavior of the waitress in the above example was stigmatizing. A range of other possible contextual options could have explained the behaviors: 1) The waitress was an immature individual; 2) she had not been trained to deal with customers; 3) she never intended to offend anyone; or 4) her job was not challenging enough. In order for the behavior to be defined as stigmatizing, other factors such as frequency and intensity would be taken into account.

Jamaicans with Disabilities

Available information on disability in Jamaica also applies to deafness. However, not much has been published. There are objective problems: "What constitutes a disability in Jamaica remains unclear, as some of the subclassifications for disability and handicap, adopted by the World Health Organization, have been found to be too complicated for our [Jamaica] setting" (Thorburn 1993b p. 1). She notes that "this particularly applies [in the case] of the 'invisible' disabilities (hearing and learning), resulting in very different perceptions of disability prevalence between professionals who measure the impairment, and the layman who perceives the outward manifestations, which, in mild cases, may not be evident". (p. 1). Consequently, the criteria used by Jamaican researchers are excerpted from the WHO Manual "Training Disabled People in the Community" and adopted by the International Epidemiological Study on Severe Childhood Disability (IESCD) in 1989 (Appendix).

Thorburn, a medical doctor working with the individuals with disabilities in Jamaica, contends that accurate information on disability in the region is lacking, as most of the research not only suffers from imprecise definitions of disability, but from a lack of information concerning the magnitude of the problem, a lack of appropriate instruments to identify and assess children, and the belief that management is difficult and expensive. Childhood disability seems to be the focus of disability research in Jamaica and, although surveys have been carried out in Jamaica and the Caribbean during the last decade, they remain unpublished. She advises that:

> The only previous published study on Jamaican attitudes and practices was on health beliefs and conducted in a group of parents who were in a community based rehabilitation program in St. Catherine in 1987. ...No extensive study of a variety of general attitudes has yet been published. (Thorburn, 1993a, p. 1)

Leavitt (1992) examined disability and rehabilitation in rural Jamaica and found that almost 60% of caregivers interviewed report and show no stigmatizing attitudes towards persons with disabilities. Seventy percent of the respondents in the study say they would not consider placing their child who is disabled in an institution. This response accounted for the presence of males living in the households as well as very strong religious beliefs and non-stigmatizing comments made by others. Leavitt's respondents were drawn from the rural population, and their children had either severe or moderate disabilities.

Thorburn points out that in Jamaica and the developing world children with mild disability, who are the largest group, are not usually perceived as "disabled." She notes that these children with disabilities are usually accepted but, as they grow older and fail to meet expectations, they sometimes receive quite brutal treatment, even by loving parents.

She argues that children with disabilities face problems arising from ignorance and negative altitudes, misunderstanding about the nature and cause of disability; the notion that their disability is a sickness, unrealistic expectations of them, pity and over protection, and feelings of shame and rejection.

Investigating the attitudes of the Jamaican community towards the disabled in the parishes of St. Catherine and St. Mary, Thorburn (1993) surveyed a stratified sample of different occupational groups for supernatural beliefs, misconceptions about disability, awareness of rights of people with disability, knowledge of services, and willingness to offer assistance to persons with disabilities. Sixty-eight percent of the respondents rejected the most negative and stigmatizing misconceptions: "not going too close to a disabled person," "disabled always a burden," "I don't like to look at," and "disabled children would not be able to work or marry." Twenty-six percent thought that persons with disabilities can be a burden sometimes, and the category, children with disabilities playing with children without disabilities," was rejected by only five percent.

Questions on equal job opportunities and the cost of services showed that only 50% of the respondents recognized the equal rights of people with disabilities to these services. Ninety-six percent of the respondents felt that programs for persons with disabilities should be shared by the government and the community, while twenty five percent felt that government should bear all costs. Thorburn found that higher frequencies of supernatural beliefs about disability came from the lower income earning occupations and from the oldest age group - fifty and over. With respect to institutionalization, the parents of children with severe mental and physical disabilities expressed a desire to place them in an institution, because there is a widespread belief that the institution is the best place.

The Role of the Jamaican Government

The government of Jamaica does not adequately provide for the welfare of Jamaicans with disabilities. In its policy statement on disability, the government admits:

> On examination of our current legislation affecting persons with disabilities, it [the current legislation] has been found to be grossly inadequate in protecting their rights, in particular their rights to housing, transportation, privacy of vote, employment and health care ... Other than the fundamental rights provided, our constitution does not specifically protect the rights of persons with disabilities. It only refers to, or makes provisions for, such persons in a few sections of the constitution. (p. 3)

The government continues:

> Jamaicans with disabilities should not in any way be restricted from fully enjoying their rights and freedoms, or from developing their total potential by the prejudices of society. Instead, they should be afforded the same opportunity

as other Jamaicans to take their proper place in society. (p. 8)

The literature suggests that during the 1980's, there was stagnation of government supported services, but that in the past three years there has been a renewal of interest and policies are now being re-examined. A Five Year Development Plan include new policy statements on education for children with disabilities. In addition, the International Convention on the Rights of the Child in 1991 has stimulated renewed efforts, and the Coalition on the Rights of the Child includes a sub-committee on children with disabilities. The Ministry of Labour and Welfare has also set up a policy/legislation advisory committee.

Jamaicans in the Deaf Culture

No research suggests that individuals who are deaf in Jamaica belong to the deaf culture. However, based on the following, there might be a deaf culture in Jamaica. First, some individuals who are deaf belong to organizations developed specifically to deal with deafness and matters concerning deafness. These organizations include schools such as the Lister Mair Gilbey School for the Deaf, the Jamaica Association for the Deaf, and various professional and other interest groups of adults who are deaf. Second, these persons share a language -- the Jamaican Sign Language -- which facilitates the development of values, socializing patterns, behaviors, perceptions, world views, humor and other factors specific to their culture. Finally, these Jamaicans who are deaf interact with their counterparts in other countries through representation at, and receipt of information from, the International Center on Deafness at Gallaudet University in Washington, D.C.

Stigma in Cultural Contexts

Monastic orders are reportedly the first groups within Christian Europe to have stressed the importance of imagery to culture and, through a process of self-stigmatization, they provided "the model for subsequent forms of stigmatization in Western history" (Solomon, 1986). This was done largely through keen attention to proper conduct and clerical appearance, for example, by shaving of the head and, bringing great attention to Christ's wounds, which are the most important stigmas in Western culture. The data indicates that, as western culture developed, "[art forms compare Christianity] to the life-giving, orderly functions of the upper body -- the heart, the head, and Christ's blood, [while] non-christian forces were being likened to the corrupting, disorderly functions of the lower body -- the sexual organs, the anus, and faeces" (Solomon, 1986 p. 63). These religious metaphors subsequently contributed to stigmatization of groups such as butchers, barbers and surgeons, who work with hair, blood and flesh within these cultures.

As subsequent stigmatizing behaviors began to express themselves among other groups in other cultures, Embree (1946) studied a peasant village, Suye Mura, in rural Japan. The researcher contended that persons with disabilities are not necessarily disqualified from a normal life. But Kojima (1977) countered that, in traditional Japanese society, normalization is not necessarily the case as protection or rejection of the person with disability depends on the local leader's attitude as well as popular opinion. She argues:

> ... the distribution of wealth was such that a disabled child born into a poor family had no future other than the expectation of dying poor. But when a malformed child was born into the rich merchant class, it was thought of as a "lucky child" (fukusuke or fukuko). Children born with large heads and fat cheeks were considered symbols of wealth and wisdom embodying all the misfortunes of the entire family. If the family mistreated the so-called "sacrifice" child, it would be punished by the gods; if it treated the child well, business would prosper. (p.23)

While the literature indicates a relationship between culture and stigma, Hanks and Hanks (1948) research on persons with disabilities in certain non-western societies represents "the first systematic anthropological treatment of physical disability to appear in the literature" (Meyerson, 1948b, p. 7). These scholars advise that the social position of disabled persons in cultures other than the United States vary. They identify five variations ranging from pariah, which, particularly in India, confers the status of persons with disabilities as being a threat to society; economic liability, which accounts for Eskimos disposing of persons with disabilities because of slim margins of surplus; tolerant utilization, by which the Northern Blackfoot of the North American Plains expect persons with disabilities to contribute in so far as they are able; limited participation, which dictates that both men with and without disabilities among the Trobriand Islanders labor to provide quantities of yams (akin to currency in this culture) for their sister and aged parents; and laissez-faire attitudes of Portuguese East Africans who shelter and provide for persons with disabilities, whether they are able to give labor or not.

In another study, Richardson et al. (1961) investigated the reactions of African American, White, and Puerto Rican children towards various types of "pictured children" with visible disabilities and found cultural uniformity in the hierarchy of preferences which the children exhibit for the "pictured children." But Jacques et al. (1970) advise that differential treatment of persons with disabilities is based on the meaning of disability within a particular culture. In investigating the attitudinal responses of nondisabled students towards persons with disabilities in Denmark, Greece and the United States, they found consistent cultural differences. They advise that most positive attitudes were found in the United States, followed by Denmark and Greece respectively. The scholars also discovered that in the United States there was no observed difference in response between males and females; in Denmark, males were more positive than females, and in Greece females were more positive than males. However, Goffman advises that, regardless of what attributes or characteristics are identified as stigmatizing in each society, a stigma is a moral taint which discredits the individual.

In a study done in Africa, Merriam (1974) reported that almost no malformed persons are found in the African village of Lupupa Ngye, except those who have lost fingers or toes through accidents. This results from the general practice of killing all malformed children (**bishuwashuwa**), midgets (**bipinji**), mongoloids (**kapalamanda**), and dwarfs (**bitesha**).

> ...two political dignitaries take the child to Mwipata, a location midway between the villages, where they kill it with a blow to the back of the head delivered by a stick. They then lecture the spirit of the child, telling it not to return to the village to cause trouble... and, albinos were killed by squeezing their chest until their ribs were broken.... (p. 21)

Groce (1985) provided another instance of the relationship between culture and attitudes towards persons with disabilities. In her study she advises that deaf island residents on Martha's Vineyard have a strong cultural tradition to support their integration, as disability is reframed as a normal human variation. The difference between persons who are hearing and persons who are not, Groce notes, is as trivial as the difference in eye color.

In another study, Ainlay et al. (1986) advised that the experience of stigma for individuals arises from social attitudes that are both subtle and pervasive and that individuals experience culturally dictated stigmas as failures to conform to society. However, Scheer and Groce (1988) concluded that while culturally shared responses to the stigma of disability vary across social contexts, relatively little attention is paid to cross cultural perspectives of this issue.

By discussing the responses of culturally diverse groups of individuals who are deaf, the present study represents an attempt to investigate whether another perspective on stigma exists.

Summary of the Literature

Much of the data confirm Goffman's assertion that stigmatization of persons with disabilities is based on the perception that the condition of disability is negatively different. Fewer studies provide data on the stigmatization of persons with disabilities in cultural contexts. Even fewer researchers who examine stigma within cultures conclude, like Ainlay and his colleagues (1986), that the underlying cultural basis for the perception of stigma may have profound consequences for the nature of stigmatization and the individual's experience of it. Further, the literature indicates dismissive attitudes towards differences in the ways individuals who are disabled deal with stigma. For example, while Sussman (1994) recognizes that "... understanding the experience of disability depends on balancing and integrating all available information" (p.20), she dismisses as "not in question" the validity of research which indicates that persons with disability claim to, at least partially, avoid negative attitudes. Sussman supports Murphy et al's (1988) assertion that persons with disabilities suffer from low self-esteem, the invasion and occupation of thought by physical defects, a strong undercurrent of anger, and the acquisition of new, total and undesirable identity.

Sussman and Murphy et al's perspective is supported by more than fifty years of research provided by other scholars, indicating an abundance of negative attitudes towards persons with disabilities. "It is unrealistic," argues von Henting (1948), "and unscientific to assume that the outer world contributes more reassuring than unsettling elements to the state of the soul of the disabled. The bias is there" (p.23). This present study suggests that because negative attitudes towards disability are so overwhelming, there is little emphasis on how persons with disabilities view their condition. Even where persons with disabilities refute the perception of negative difference and become politically militant, their effort is minimized. Goffman criticizes:

> When the ultimate political objective is to remove the stigma from the differentness, the individual may find that his very efforts can politicize his own life, rendering it even more different from the normal life initially denied him. (pp. 116 -124)

The present study notes some of these paradigms which Fine and Asch (1988) identify. They suggest, for example, that Dworkin and Dworkin (1976) indicate "...selection of the relevant characteristics upon which identifiability is based is neither fixed nor self-evident; rather, it is variable and socially defined and interpreted" (p. 18). They also identify Hanks and Hanks

(1948) and Schulz and Decker (1985) as being among researchers who "reframe disability as a minority group issue in which a set of socially negotiated meanings of the body are played out psychologically, socially and politically" (p. 18). In addition, Meyerson (1988) recognizes as "solid gain," Shontz's (1977) propositions for disability research (p. 185). Shontz's studies contribute to viewing disability not primarily in damaged bodies, but in the political/social/legal system that denies equal protection of the law, equal rights and equal opportunities. (Meyerson, 1988 p. 185)

Fine and Asch (1988) also suggest that much of the literature is locked in narrow assumptions about people with disabilities. They claim that researchers assume that: 1) disability is located solely in biology (Katz, 1981; Kleck, 1969); 2) impairment causes problems (Jones et al. 1984); 3) disabled persons are victims (Bulman and Wortman, 1977); 4) disability is central to the disabled person's self concept, self-definition, social comparisons, and reference groups (Taylor et al. 1983; Jones et al. 1984); and 5) having a disability is synonymous with needing help and social support. (Brickman et al., 1982; Deutsch, 1985)

The literature also indicates that Goffman's perspective continues to be the main reference on stigma. Sussman (1994) informs that the literature does not indicate any substantial challenge to Goffman's theory that adverse responses to persons with disabilities, unfavorable images of them, and their own negative self-valuations are explained -- when they exist -- by perceptions of negative difference.

This study also recognizes the importance of other sociological and psychological theories on stigma identified in the literature but submits that the field of intercultural communication should conduct research to derive its generic theoretical perspective on stigma. "Clearly," argue Ainlay and his colleagues, "[different theoretical] perspectives all contribute something to our understanding of the development of stigmatization ... [but] just as clearly they differ in emphasis" (p. 190). The present study does not develop an intercultural communication theory of stigma but provides data and working hypotheses which might be valuable in explaining and understanding how individuals who are deaf cope with stigma. The researcher now discusses the theoretical framework that guides this study.

Chapter 3

Theoretical Framework

Assumptions of Intercultural Communication

Dodd (1991) advises that, where cultural variability enters communication, it is called intercultural communication, and he lists four assumptions which guide the study of intercultural communication. First, interculturalists assume that the perception of differences exists between cultures and that people do not necessarily share norms, practices, and beliefs. It is, therefore, the bridging of the intercultural gap that gives intercultural communication its fullest meaning. On this basis, this study argues that members of the hearing society may perceive individuals, who may or may not regard themselves as part of the deaf culture, as negatively different. When this occurs, the individual who is deaf and belonging to the deaf culture might not necessarily agree with the perception. As previously discussed, the data indicate that individuals who consider themselves part of the deaf culture do not regard deafness as an inability nor as negatively different (Jankowski, 1991).

Second, intercultural communication is the basis of social relationships which affect how messages are interpreted. This researcher argues that cultures interact because of social, economic, political, and cultural necessity and that this interaction affects the relationships between cultures. The study submits that, with reference to the deaf culture, stigmatizing attitudes develop in the course of the interaction between deaf and hearing cultures.

Third, the cognitive, social, and communication styles of individuals affect intercultural communication. This study contends that both hearing and deaf cultures not only use different communication styles but entirely different languages. English language is the first language of the hearing culture, while Sign Language is the first of the deaf culture. The literature indicates that members of the deaf culture in the United States use the English Language as their second language in speechreading, reading and writing. As well, some members of the hearing culture also use Sign Language as their second language in their interaction with members of the deaf culture. This study suggests that one way for communication difficulties to be reduced is for both cultures to respect and learn each other's language.

Kim (1988; 1989) argues from an Adaptation theoretical perspective, suggesting that adaptation to each other's culture is a cumulative process, whereby individuals gradually and incrementally adapt to their environment. She notes that, for successful adaptation to take place, there must be, among other variables, knowledge of the language, acculturation motivation, positive attitudes, and participation in interpersonal networks.

Fourth, intercultural communication depends upon reducing uncertainty levels about other people. The theory of uncertainty reduction was developed by Berger and Calabrese (1975) and extended by Gudykunst and Kim (1984) and Gudykunst (1988). It focusses on the concept of "stranger," who experiences uncertainty and anxiety on entering new cultural relationships. In relation to both hearing and deaf cultures, this study speculates that in communication interactions members of both cultures become 'strangers' to each other, and they are uncertain about what to expect, and how to behave. The theory of uncertainty reduction suggests further that, for uncertainty to be reduced, both cultures must change personal expectations, reduce cognitive uncertainty, and alter their anxieties. The present study posits that the hearing culture, for example, might need to change its personal expectation that, because members of the deaf culture do not hear, they are consequently dumb. The individual who is deaf, on the other hand, must change his or her expectation that the hearing culture's responses will be negative.

This study suggests one way in which uncertainty about the deaf culture may be reduced. Researchers should provide the literature with more information on the deaf culture -- data on how they view themselves, how they view their disability, how they view members of the hearing culture, how they feel social interaction may be improved, and how they should be treated by the hearing culture. It is hoped that the present study may assist in addressing these issues.

The Rules Perspective and Coordinated Management of Meaning

Dodd (1991) notes that every culture has a fundamental set of expectations about how things are to be accomplished. These are called rules or procedures. "Most people are aware of the way we are expected to perform in a culture. Unfortunately, the rules of a culture are rarely stated; nevertheless, we are expected to develop communication competence with those rules" (p. 53). Shimanoff (1980) defines a rule as a followable prescription that indicates what behavior is obligated, preferred, or prohibited in certain contexts. In order for a rule to be followable, she asserts that an individual must have the option to follow or violate a rule. When there is no choice, then the rule is not followable. Rules become prescriptive when an individual fails to abide by a rule and can be criticized for this action. She argues that, contextually, a rule must do more than govern a single event but, at the same time, cannot govern everything. She advises that rules specify appropriate behavior, guiding individuals to make choices between what is to be done and what is not to be done. Finally, she describes the 'if-then' variable: the 'if' clause specifies the nature of the prescription, and the 'then' clause specifies the behavior.

The theory of the Coordinated Management of Meaning (Pearce and Cronen 1980) discusses another perspective on rules. Littlejohn (1992) provides a comprehensive summary of the theory of Co-ordinated Management of Meaning (CMM), which views people as acting on the basis of constitutive (rules of meaning) and regulative rules (rules of action) to understand and interpret the events they experience. He advises that rules of meaning and action are chosen within a context which is the frame of reference for interpreting an action. The researcher mentions four typical contexts which are interrelated: relationship -- including mutual expectations among group members; episode, which is the event; self, comprising one's sense of personal definition; and, archetype, which reflects perception of general truth. He contends that these contexts are only typical, as humans have the ability to create a number of contexts for interpreting and acting on any event or text. Sometimes, text and context form a loop, and, where the interpretation rules are consistent throughout the loop, Littlejohn advises that the loop is said to be charmed or self-confirmatory.

He summarizes that rules provide a logical force for behaviors as people behave in a manner consistent with their rules. He identifies four types of logical force operating in communication. Prefigurative or causal force,

Littlejohn posits, is that which allows a prior condition to compel individuals to behave in specific ways. Practical force, he notes, is that series of 'oughts' that guide interpretations, responses and actions, and which cause individuals to behave in certain ways to achieve a future condition. Contextual force is the third type, and, as individuals believe that action and interpretation are a natural part of the context, this refers to a pressure from the context to act. Finally, he indicates that as individuals create new contexts or change existing ones, they use implicative force to do so.

Coordination vs Coorientation

CMM theorists advance the thesis that human communication is inherently imperfect and "that people can have perfectly satisfactory coordination without understanding one another" (Littlejohn, p. 207). "...the ideal of perfect mutual understanding is not only unattainable, it is an unreasonable goal. Not all acts of communication are intentional or purposeful, so co-orientation, or mutual understanding, is not required. The goal of communication is ...coordination -- the pattern of interaction that makes sense and is coherent to participants [and]... the management of meanings occurs when meanings are assigned to messages within interaction, and that assignment is based on an interpretive, unique message for each participant" (Dodd, 1991 p. 26). Littlejohn concurs:

> The primary task in all communication...is to achieve and then sustain some form of coordination [which] involves meshing one's actions with those of another to the point of feeling that the sequence of actions is logical or appropriate. The communicators in an exchange need not interpret the events in the same way, but each must feel, from within his or her own system of rules, that what is happening makes sense - that is the essence of co-ordination. (p. 33)

Based on the theory of Coordinated Management of Meaning, this study contends both hearing and deaf cultures do not have to agree on whether or not deafness is a negative condition. However, they achieve coordination when each culture feels that, within its own system of rules, its beliefs and behaviors are logical.

This study departs theoretically from Goffman's sociological approach to stigma by adopting the rules perspective in its analysis. Goffman's work was centered on attribution theory which focusses on the ways people infer causes of behavior. Littlejohn (1991) lists the main assumptions of this theory:

First, people attempt to determine the causes of behavior. When in doubt, they look for information that will help them answer the question, Why is she doing that? ... the second assumption of attribution theory is that people assign causes systematically ... and third ... the attributed cause has impact on the perceiver's own feelings and behavior. The communicator's attributions determine in large part the meaning for the situation. (pp.139-140)

This study submits that attributions are imposed perceptions and that, without interaction to provide an alternative frame of reference, such perceptions become standardized.

The Concept of Personal Communication World View

Although members of the deaf culture may use rules of meaning and rules of action to make choices in responding to stigmatizing behaviors, as individuals they may also hold their unique world views which relate to their communication environments. An individual's personal communication world view (PCWV), "...assumes that individuals adopt from their cultures and from their personalities a system of thinking about the amount of control, influence, choice, and regulation they can exert in their communication climates" (Dodd, 1991 p. 83). Dodd advises that individuals can have either a high communication control (HCC) or a low communication control (LCC). He notes that a HCC individual finds choices and decisions easy to make and "exhibits a communication style consistent with the personal communication world view that shows statistically significant linkage with openness, low communication apprehension, innovativeness, high self-esteem, organizational co-operation, cognitive complexity, and opinion leadership" (p. 83). He advises that LCC individuals express opposite attitudes and behaviors as well as expressing little control over their communication climates.

Recognizing that individuals have a personal orientation system, Klopf (1987) notes that humans are predisposed to behave in certain ways and that these predispositions, which are made up of needs, values, beliefs and attitudes, control one's conduct in society. He advises that these predispositions are learned within the framework of a specific culture and that needs are primary as they activate communication behavior. Maslow (1943) presents a hierarchy of needs: physiological, which relate to self preservation; safety, accounting for the need to be safe from danger; love, requiring acceptance by others; esteem, desiring respect from others; and, self-actualization -- desiring to reach the height of one's personal abilities. In subsequent research Hofstede (1984) recognizes relevance of Maslow's theory to intercultural communication but indicates that needs vary from culture to culture. This study posits that needs as well as values may vary from individual to individual. Klopf notes that values are the evaluative facets which help individuals to determine what is right or wrong, good or bad and he cites two rules of value applicable to intercultural situations: "The first is that each participant in an intercultural transaction should understand the other's values...the second..implies respect for the other's values..." . (p. 80)

Against this background, this study returns to its research questions as they relate to the communication theory of Coordinated Management of Meaning (CMM) and the concept of Personal World View: (1) What links, if any, can be demonstrated among culture, stigma, and deafness? (2) What constitutive or regulative rules may be derived for selected deaf populations for dealing with stigmatization?

The literature suggests that communication and culture are inseparable (Smith, 1966; Hecht et al, 1989); communication is culture and culture is communication (Hall, 1959); the way people communicate is the way they live. It is their culture (Klopf, 1987); and reality within a culture is defined by individual and complex acts, but how that reality is understood is determined by the conventions of communication at the time (Gergen, 1985). This researcher proposes that there might be a link between stigma, deafness and culture. She believes that stigma, as the convergence of perceptions, is the reality attributed to deafness and communicated to and accepted by the bearers of the condition. She believes further that, as perception, stigma becomes a construct in an individual's cognitive schema, and Littlejohn notes that culture influences the types of constructs held by individuals. In addition, Kelly (1955) and Applegate and Sypher (1983; 1988) create a theory of personal constructs, and, although it is a cognitive approach, "...it recognizes at base that constructs have social origins, they are learned through interaction with other people ... [are a] direct result of a history of interaction in [cultural] groups, and cannot be divorced from social life" (Littlejohn, 1991 pp. 119-120). Littlejohn advises that constructs are organized into interpretive schemes, which identify what something is and place the object in a category. He contends that a construct is a distinction between opposites and, that by classifying an experience into categories, the individual gives meaning to the experience.

This study provides the following hypothetical examples to speculate how constitutive and regulative rules might be used by selected deaf populations in contending with the perception of negative difference.

The Jamaican Group

As previously noted, the present study speculates that Jamaicans who are deaf and who might consider themselves part of a deaf culture are in the high context culture of Jamaica and mainly in a working class culture resulting from economic class divisions. This researcher questions whether these individuals would not operate from the following perspectives in the hypothetical examples below:

> Perspective A -- Individuals who are deaf communicate differently and are in a culture by themselves. Since deaf individuals do not hear and must communicate with the hearing, the hearing culture should be sensitive to this communication difference. Such sensitivity may express itself in "good works" such as patience, understanding, and learning sign language.

> Perspective B -- Messages are not always specific. How messages are interpreted depend on the context of not only the message, but also of the interaction.

Mary is twenty-two years old and deaf. Her parents are finding it increasingly difficult to support her financially, so she decides to visit Mr. Charles at his grocery store to seek any available type of employment. Mr. Charles perceives that her deafness makes her unable to perform and communicates to her that he is very sorry but, if only she could hear, he would be happy to find something for her to do. However, instinct for "good works" is important in the Jamaican culture so he advises her that she should not worry but should visit him from time to time for food and donations.

Mary then uses a combination of constitutive and regulative rules, along with her own personal communication world view, to interpret this event and determine her behavior. First, her constitutive cultural rules may allow her to interpret Mr. Charles' response as "You are deaf and deaf people are not fit to work. Go, home." The hierarchy of needs in her PCWV influence her regulative rule behavior. If her physiological need for food is most important and the event will allow for that need to be met, she might react in a manner that might appear to agree with Mr. Charles' thesis. If the need for self-actualization is most important, she might urge Mr. Charles to allow her to prove her capabilities.

There are several scenarios within the various contexts of this interaction: Relationship context -- Mr. Charles, a hearing person, expects Mary, who is deaf, to agree that deaf persons are not employable. If Mary agrees that this is so, based on the working class rules of the culture, she expects Mr. Charles to be sensitive and do "good." If she does not accept that this is so, she expects Mr. Charles (also based on the rules of the culture) to "have a heart" and allow her to show what she can do. Her responses would also relate to her definition of self in the self-concept context. When she defines herself as deaf and unable to function effectively, she would tend to be submissive. On the other hand, if she regards herself as capable, she would tend to more actively resist the perception of negative difference. Within the archetype context, Mary might compare herself to other members of the deaf culture. If she can find no other employed member of the deaf culture, she might conclude that it is generally true that persons who are deaf ought not to be employed. If she identifies other persons who are deaf in gainful employment, she might choose courses of action to support her claims that members of the deaf culture can function in job situations.

There are several forces operating in Mary's interaction with Mr. Charles: prefigurative, wherein she perceives that, were she not a person who is deaf, she would not be faced with this situation; practical, wherein she recognizes that she "ought" to agree with Mr. Charles' assessment or face his impatience and not receive his "good works;" contextual, wherein she believes that Mr. Charles' reaction to deny her employment was logical and natural; or implicative, where she could try to change Mr. Charles' attitude towards the employment of people who are deaf in that community. As a result of this interaction, coordination occurs as both parties have interacted in a way that they understand each other. Mary either understands that people who are deaf are not fit to be employed or that they should be given an opportunity to prove themselves. Mr. Charles either understands that he has made himself clear that he will not employ an individual who is deaf and that Mary will not re-raise the issue or that he will give her an opportunity to do something and, if she does it well, he will consider employing her.

Mary Interacts With a Hearing Person from Perspective B:

Mary goes to church on Sunday. She is the only person who is deaf in the young adults association. The pastor needs someone to be in charge of the church's child-care facility during the sermon delivery on Sundays. Every member of the young adult association must have a responsibility and, when Mary volunteers, the pastor eagerly obliges.

Mary does a good job and the parishioners who are satisfied with the quality care given at the facility, ask that the service be offered full time and a paid employee recruited. The pastor does not offer Mary the position but employs a hearing person.

Mary will now have to examine the context of the pastor's action to determine whether or not she had been stigmatized. These are possible options: 1) The pastor could have felt that forty hours of work per week would have been too stressful for her, and by not offering her the job he had been acting in her best interest; 2) she had never indicated that she wanted a full time job and therefore he did not think she would have been interested; 3) the new employee had been volunteering in the church even before Mary joined; and 4) maybe he did not think that, as a person who was deaf, she could manage the challenges of a full time job.

Whichever option Mary selects will depend on the availability of information within the context to support it. For example, if she chooses option one, she would perhaps recall instances where the pastor had to recommend that she take leave after she had worked consistently for eight hours. She could conclude that he cared about her health. If she chooses the last option, she may question why she was able enough to take care of the children as a volunteer and not as a salaried employee. She then concludes that she has been stigmatized.

Realizing that she has been stigmatized, Mary's constitutive rule may allow her to interpret the action as "You are deaf. You could not answer the telephone and take messages. It wouldn't work out." But, after prioritizing her needs in her PCWV, she decides that self-actualization is high on her agenda. Using her regulative rules, she insists that she should have been offered the job, and confronts the pastor's communal instincts by suggesting that it would be nice for him to offer her the job since she had been doing such a fine job as a volunteer. She expects the pastor to accept her suggestion and treat her as he would a hearing person.

If she interprets the pastor's action as negative and if she lacks self-confidence, her need to avoid embarrassment will be central in her PCWV. Thus, she might agree that she would have difficulties in the job. In each case, the context of self-confidence is important as personal definition also affects the choices made. She may also seek 'general truths' about the deaf culture from the archetype context. If few are gainfully employed, she may be more confident to join the workforce; if many are employed, she may view her own employment as a natural activity; if none is employed, she may challenge the pastor for employment so she can be a model to her colleagues.

There are also different types of operative forces in this interaction: prefigurative, wherein she either perceives herself as worthy of the job, or wherein she perceives accepting it would end in her being a failure; practical, wherein she recognizes that she ought to be given the job since she is a good worker; contextual, wherein she perceives the pastor making an incorrect assumption; or implicative, wherein accepting the job would improve the employment image of persons who are deaf. Coordination occurs when the pastor, in spite of his own reservations, allows Mary to prove herself; and, when Mary understands that as a person who is deaf, she is not bound by her deafness to make uncomfortable choices and accept stigmatizing behaviors.

In both interactions, the influence of culture, rules and personal communication world view choices allow for resistance to possible stigmatizing behaviors. Based on the individuals needs and rules employed, any choice or combination of choices could have been made.

This study questions if, in the Jamaican context, responses to stigmatizing behaviors fluctuate on a continuum between the simultaneous operation of perspective A and perspective B. This situation might also exist because there is an insufficiency of legal guidelines to regulate interaction between the deaf and hearing cultures; hence negotiation as a strategy is often employed. Where members of the deaf culture choose to reject perceptions of negative difference, this study speculates that deafness is not necessarily a negative experience.

Following is a hypothetical example of rule guided behaviors of an African American who is Deaf:

Mayo is a forty-five year old African American professor who is deaf and who works at an American College for the Deaf. He visits the model unit in an upscale neighborhood, with a view to purchasing a home. The white sales clerk looks at him, asks him a question and realizes that he is both Black and deaf. She perceives that his disability will pose a problem to the members of the neighborhood. She leafs through her files and tells him that unfortunately her assistant sold the last unit that afternoon.

Mayo is accustomed to receiving negative responses, but his constitutive and regulative rules dictate how he interprets and copes with stigmatizing behaviors. The sales clerk expects him to understand that there are no more units available and he expects of himself to challenge this report. As a member of a low context culture, he asks her directly if his color and deafness factored into her remarks. She says, "Oh, No!"

That same afternoon, he asks his wife to visit the unit. She is white and hearing. The sales clerk takes her on a tour of the three remaining units and accepts her deposit. Mayo returns with his wife and using the rules of his lr w context culture, he confronts the sales clerk and identifies her behavior as stigmatizing. Mayo realizes that he is facing a double stigma but is not sure which is operating. He researches the race of the new home owners and finds that equal amounts of African Americans and Whites live there. His constitutive rules interpret that the stigma was his deafness. He now has to decide whether to accept this stigmatizing behavior or challenge it. He does the latter because 1) he has the legal right to live in that community; 2) he wants to live there; 3) his culture has legal protection against discrimination; the sales clerk violated his rights.

In his PCWV, his need for cultural accessibility to basic human need is paramount. Mayo determines his course of action and takes legal action against the clerk and the housing developer. He wins a multimillion dollar settlement but, most importantly to him, the deaf culture claims this as a new victory. The legal system of American society facilitates the deaf culture defending its rights. In every context where the stigmas of race and deafness confront African Americans who are deaf, this study speculates that they make choices based on the rules of interpretation and action as well as their own personal communication world view.

The following is a hypothetical example of rule guided behaviors of a White American who is Deaf:

Susan is white and deaf. She works as a library assistant and collects request slips from readers at the information desk. She is organizing the slips and does not hear that a white reader has been tapping on the desk for assistance. She turns around to take another slip when she notices him standing there, looking very angry. She lip reads and realizes that he is calling her a deaf dummy. Her constitutive rule allows her to interpret his actions as stigmatizing, and her regulative rules suggest that she confront this behavior. There is no interracial conflict, and she decides that gender is not the issue. The issue is one of deafness and Susan is firmly against being stigmatized. She takes a pen and scribbles a note which she passes to him. It reads, "Go to hell!" If he reports her to her supervisor, the clarity of the issue allows her to develop appropriate strategies.

The scenario is repeated with an African American male who is hearing. He calls her a deaf dummy. She uses her constitutive rules to interpret his behavior. She concludes that the issue is deafness but has to choose whether or not to accept stigmatizing behaviors from another stigmatized person. The issue of race is thus introduced. She is angry. "A gorilla has just uttered his first word!" she says to herself. She uses her regulative rules and chooses to reject the behavior. Pretending not to understand him, she smiles at him and walks away to the rest room where she spends the next fifteen minutes doing nothing. She returns to the desk and he is still standing there, unaware that she has just made a fool of him. He is irate and demands to see the supervisor. The issues are deafness, race, and gender. Her constitutive rules remove the issue of gender. It is difficult for her to separate the issue of race because of traditional interracial conflict between African Americans and Whites. Confronting stigmatizing behaviors from African Americans therefore introduces a racial element in deafness. When race and deafness are both introduced, the individual uses constitutive and regulative rules to assign priority.

Susan's personal communication world view influences any decision she makes. If respect for herself as a member of the deaf culture had been paramount, Susan could have used rules from her low context culture to ask both men why they had chosen to react negatively to her deafness. If receiving negative responses from an African American had been intolerable, Susan could have introduced the issue of race. As with the African American and Jamaican Deaf cultures, responses to stigmatizing behaviors might be determined by the rules used and choices made.

Summary

The present study proposes that the Coordinated Management of Meaning as a Rules theory within the interpretive paradigm affords the best framework to examine (a) the possible links between stigma, deafness, and culture and (b) the constitutive and regulative rules that selected deaf populations use in dealing with stigmatization. The theory details that a relationship exists between cultural context, interpretation of messages, and behavior, and thus allows this study to theoretically depart from Goffman's nomothetic conclusion that deafness is a stigmatizing and negative condition.

The Concept of Personal Communication World View discussed in the study provides the framework to analyze the role of choices which individuals make in the communication process. Both the Coordinated Management of Meaning and the Concept of Personal Communication World view offer a perspective to understand that groups and individuals are not passive receivers of attributions but are interactive in the process of intercultural communication.

The present study also recognizes that the theoretical framework facilitates the methodology, as answers to the research questions emerge from the voices of deaf persons themselves, and not from a sociological theory which allows hearing individuals to decide how deaf individuals feel about deafness. The methodological framework of the study will now be discussed.

Chapter 4

Research Design and Methodology

This intercultural communication study is guided by a qualitative research method which shares the metatheoretical assumptions of the interpretive paradigm. "[A] paradigm," advises Lindlof (1995), "has come to mean simply a coherent set of assumptive beliefs, theoretic propositions, constructs, modes of inference, and domains of subject matter" (p.30). In addition, Lindlof suggests that "a paradigm becomes dominant ... because of its ability to account for empirical reality and also because of its fecundity of problems to be solved" (p.29). The interpretive paradigm adopted by this study assumes that people create and sustain social reality through their subjective and intersubjective experience. Thus, this study finds this paradigm useful in explaining and understanding how the deaf culture negotiates and interprets its symbolic activities in the process of communicating with the hearing culture. The paradigm also explains how such symbolic activities are determined by the cultural life of the deaf.

The present study notes, however, that the interpretive paradigm has been criticized for its inability to generalize its findings, to predict the future, as well as for conducting only few empirical studies (Infante et al 1990). Kuhn (1970) is critical: "[Paradigms are] universally recognized scientific achievements that for a time provide model problems and solutions to a community of practitioners" (p. viii). This researcher adopts the interpretive paradigm not as a method, but rather as a coherent way of studying communication. It subjectively focusses on the interaction of individuals within the context of their interaction (Lindlof 1995). The interpretive paradigm and "scientific method" are incommensurable approaches to the study of communication; each responds to a different ontology.

Lindlof (1995) discusses some of the principles of the interpretive paradigm. First, social situations must be viewed from the perspective of the social actors in order to understand what is happening in that situation. The interpretive paradigm "takes understanding as its principal topic and as the wellspring of its methodology" (p.30). Second, it "emphasizes intersubjectivity relating to 'how' a human being [learns] to construct a life world that can be shared with other human beings...[and what accounts for] so much continuity of meaning in people's actions..." (p.33). The paradigm recognizes that actions are geared together with respect to a common system of relevance. In addition, it focusses on act, action, and motive, and suggests that an action can be understood either when such an action has been completed or in an understanding of its purpose. Lindlof concludes that "we gain insight into people's motives for action by engaging them through their acts, primarily, acts of speaking. We do this," he claims, "[to identify] ... *in order to* motives e.g., 'I joined the Army to see the world' and *because* motives e.g. 'I joined the Army because I was unhappy' " (p. 34).

Focus Groups as a Method of Instrumentation

Consequent to the nature of the study and the information required to test the assumptions, the study proposes focus groups as a method of instrumentation allowing for the collection of data in the naturally occurring discourse of deaf interactants. "Focus groups create settings in which diverse perceptions, judgements and experiences concerning particular topics can surface...the ways they support, debate, or resolve issues with each other can resemble the dynamics of everyday social discourse" (Lindlof, 1995 p. 174). Stewart and Shamdasani (1990) note that focus groups do the following:

1. Provide data from a group of people much more quickly and at less cost than would be the case if each individual were interviewed separately. The members can also be assembled on much shorter notice than would be required for a more systematic, and larger survey;

2. Allow the researcher to interact directly with respondents, thereby providing opportunities for clarification, follow up questions, and for the probing of responses. In addition, the researcher can observe nonverbal responses such as gestures, smiles or frowns which may carry information that supplements or

contradicts the verbal response;

3. Provide an opportunity for the researcher to obtain large and rich amounts of data in the respondents' own words in the open response format. The researcher can therefore obtain deeper levels of meaning, make important connections, and identify subtle nuances in expression and meanings;

4. Allow respondents to react and to build upon the responses of other group members. This may result in the production of data or ideas that might not have been uncovered in individual interviews;

5. Provide flexibility to examine a wide range of topics with a variety of individuals and in a variety of settings;

6. Allow for the collection of data from children or from adults who are not particularly literate;

7. Provide easy comprehension of the results as opposed to more sophisticated survey research that employs complex statistical analyses. (p. 17)

Focus groups were first used in the valuation of audience responses to radio programs during the early 1940's and have been used for a variety of purposes since (Stewart and Shamdasani, 1990). With respect to disability research, scholars including Frank (1988), Schneider (1988), and Mest (1988) have used qualitative methods to get in-depth interview data on disability from persons with disabilities themselves, and the information gathered in these studies raises important issues for disability research. Frank notes that his interviewees' adaptations suggest some limitations to the applicability of Goffman's theory in a changing social context. Schneider asks, if disability is a social construction and has such costs, how it can best be constructed for all concerned. And Mest finds that, although persons with disabilities recognize being "different" in terms of the labels applied to them by others, they do not use those same labels when defining themselves or choosing their own friends.

The study notes that focus groups "continue to be perceived as a marketing research tool or as an exploratory technique..." (Lindlof, p.175), but they provide the best format for collecting unedited data.

Research Questions

Two research questions guide this study: (1) What links, if any, can be demonstrated among deafness, stigma, and culture? (2) What constitutive or regulative rules may be derived from selected deaf populations for dealing with stigmatization?

Sample Description

The study involved four focus groups, with a total of two representing the Jamaican deaf culture, and one each representing the African American and White American deaf cultures. The groups in Jamaica each contained nine persons while the White American and African American groups each contained six persons. All four groups were comprised of volunteers. The Jamaicans were students at the Lister Mair Gilbey School for the Deaf and were between eighteen and nineteen years old. They were senior students who were accepted for participation because of their maturity and ability to process information. These students were children of working class parents and families. The first group contained two males and seven females, while the second group was comprised of five females and four males. The African American group contained two females and four males who were students at Gallaudet University in Washington D.C. They were between the ages of nineteen and twenty-two and represented a cross section of disciplines at the University. The White American group contained five females and one male, and were also between the ages of nineteen and twenty-two. These students also represented a cross-section of disciplines at the University. The volunteers were recruited from Gallaudet as it is the world's primary liberal arts college for the deaf and also because the researcher assumed that at the college level the students would be mature and able to process information. Although more volunteers had been sought from among the African American and White American groups, only the six students in each group attended. However, the researcher felt the samples adequate as "a sample of six to twelve persons ... who have certain experiences in common" (Lindlof, 1995 p. 174) is generally accepted as sufficient. It is important to note that the informants in all four focus groups represent individuals who belong to educational institutions for the deaf and that these institutions emphasize behaviors and attitudes which affect the informants' perception of themselves as belonging to a deaf culture. The study, therefore, speculates that cultural awareness may be more emphasized among these groups than among others who do not share such reinforcement.

Recruiting the Sample

The Jamaican informants were recruited by the principal of the Lister Mair Gilbey School for the Deaf. The researcher made the initial contact with the principal by telephone. The research guide was discussed and the principal asked for volunteers from among the student body. The prospective participants were told that they would be expected to participate for one hour and that participation was voluntary. Two meetings were scheduled for one hour each in the school's auditorium. The research guide was discussed in detail with the principal in a follow-up telephone call and she held further discussions with the students. The researcher recorded the names of the students and the scheduled meeting time. The list included the names of two other students who were scheduled to participate in the event of last minute cancellations.

The American informants were recruited by this researcher with the assistance of the Dean of the School of Communication and various other staff members at Gallaudet University. The researcher and staff members visited the students in the snack bar and distributed leaflets inviting them to participate. The students were also recruited by e-mail and through the Student Body Organization. Six African American students attended and the session was held in the conference room of Dawes House. It lasted one hour and was interpreted by a certified African American Sign Language interpreter. However, due to lack of attendance, four scheduled sessions with the White American students were canceled.

The researcher and white interpreter found it necessary to visit the snack bar where the sessions were held with the White students who consented. Although the White female interpreter was not certified, her years of using sign language in communicating with the deaf contributed to her ability to interpret the session. Prior to the discussion, several attempts had been made to get a certified White American interpreter from the interpreting services at Gallaudet. On two occasions, a certified White American male interpreter attended to interpret the sessions. On one occasion, only two White American students attended and the session had to be canceled. On the other occasion, none attended. Subsequently, another session was scheduled but no one attended.

Another attempt was made to get the students and they did not attend, so the researcher decided to visit the snack bar where the students lunch at Gallaudet and have the discussion with some of the White American students. She applied to the interpreting services at Gallaudet for the services of a White American interpreter and was told that no one could be made available at that time. She contacted Deaf Pride and Arthur Richmond's Interpreting Services for interpreting services, but her calls were not returned. The services of a non-certified interpreter were then engaged. Whether certification in signing became an important variable in the research remains unclear. None of the respondents commented on the interpreter's qualifications or skill level.

Identification of Moderator

This researcher, aided by an interpreter, assumed the role of moderator. The literature suggests that a focus group moderator should combine disciplined detachment with understanding and empathy, be alert to indications that the group atmosphere is disintegrating, encourage intensive personal involvement, not appear to be artificial, and be aware that sensitive areas will frequently produce superficial rather than in depth responses. To stimulate interest and participation the researcher informed the groups before the meeting of the general topic of the interview.

Conducting the Group

One of the first responsibilities of the researcher was to create an environment in which the participants felt comfortable and free to express themselves without concern for how others felt about their opinions. Members of each group had already known each other, and this helped to reduce their uncertainties of what to expect. They were then seated around a table, allowing for maximum eye contact with each other. The moderator and interpreter were also at the table. The researcher introduced herself as well as discussed the purpose of the study and then asked for their full co-operation.

Questionnaire

Four areas of questions in the interview guide were generated in discussions with the researcher and members of the Academic Committee. The researcher was advised to consider developing questions in the following general categories: 1) who communicates with whom; 2) what communication means to individuals who are deaf; 3) how they manage communication; 4) what choices they make in communicating; 5) what stigma means; 6) what deaf culture means; 7) implicit/explicit ways they are stigmatized; and 8) their responses to stigmatizing behaviors.

The first group which held discussions with the moderator was from Jamaica. Before the scheduled time of the meeting, the moderator held an informal discussion with the group and asked them to respond to the questions. The moderator posed the same questions which had been discussed with the

Academic Committee. When the session began, the questions were posed once again, and the researcher observed that themes which had surfaced in the preliminary discussions were once again developing. These were: 1) definition of the deaf culture and behaviors within that culture; 2) the role of authority figures in the management of stigma; 3) their expectations of the hearing community; and 4) choices they make in communicating. Although not a theme, much of the discussion also centered on definition of stigma and anecdotes of stigmatizing behaviors. The researcher had to restrict the discussion of these anecdotes as the participants were very enthusiastic to report all their experiences. This would have needed more time and such discussions were not the entire focus of the study.

The second group of Jamaicans also had similar themes emerging but, in addition, focussed on sexual harassment of deaf women. The researcher re-grouped the questions according to the emerging themes in an effort to maximize the output of data in each theme. The questions were re-grouped as follows: 1) What do you understand by the term stigma? 2) Explain stigmatizing experiences you may have had. 3) How do you know if you are being stigmatized? 4) What does the term 'deaf culture' mean to you? 5) How do you respond to stigma as a group? 6) How do you feel about deafness? 7) Do you make any choices before communicating with the hearing? 8) What are these choices? 9) How do you communicate with hearing people? Based on the unsolicited response of the first group that authority figures influence them to ignore stigmatizing behaviors and that they wished hearing people would learn sign language, the researcher posed these additional questions to the second group: 10) Are you influenced in any way when deciding how to respond to stigmatizing behaviors? 11) Do you have any expectations of the hearing people in Jamaica?

Again, the interactants were eager to give anecdotes of their stigmatizing experiences with hearing individuals. The discussions were held in the school's auditorium and, as the researcher served them lunch after the meeting, members of both groups continued the discussions. Discussions with the principal and interpreter on the information derived from the focus group discussions revealed that the groups interviewed represented individuals from stable homes and family life, in which respect for authority was important. The researcher was advised that as the students shared the same basic lifestyle of attending school, going to church, and spending time with each other, they had similar experiences which could have accounted for the emergence of the themes and similarity in responses. The principal said that, if the same questions were asked of the deaf youngsters who did not attend school but gathered on the streets, responses would be different. This could be a topic for future research but this study speculates that the "street culture" could account for different attitudes toward stigma. The researcher could not account for the difference between both groups in the present study on the issue of sexual harassment.

The African American group was the next to be interviewed. These discussions took place approximately one month after the meeting with the Jamaicans, as the researcher had to await approval from the Institutional Review Board at Gallaudet to conduct the interviews. The interactants were given a list of the questions posed to the Jamaicans along with a flier inviting them to attend the session when they were first recruited. Following the introductions at the beginning of the session, the researcher first asked the informants to define 'stigma.' They reported that they had never heard the term but, in reporting their experience of it, identified white deaf Americans as the most stigmatizing group. That was the first theme to emerge from the discussion. As with the Jamaican groups, the emergent themes were very obvious in the discussions and they were also similar to those of the Jamaicans. These were behaviors within the context of the deaf culture and the choices they made in communicating. Behaviors within the low context culture was not a dominant theme but emerged when the researcher analyzed the data.

The fourth group to be interviewed was comprised of White Americans who were deaf. Once again, the themes emerged early in the discussion. With this group the dominant theme was its identification as belonging to the deaf culture. Next was the theme of interenthnic relationships with the African American deaf. Not so dominant was the theme of behaviors within the low context culture. Two respondents introduced the issues of "religion and deafness" and "women and deafness" but the information was not sufficient to constitute a theme.

The moderator's judgement was crucial in posing the questions, answers to which were interrelated. During all the discussions, the moderator paid close attention to ensuring participation, time management, problems such as members of the group wishing to leave for various reasons (e.g. to make a telephone call), and generally to the group's comfort. The moderator sought to guard against moderator bias by ensuring to probe for contrary sentiments as well as to those members who found it difficult to articulate a favorable thought. For example, in the discussions with the White American group, one respondent was reluctant to say what her anger was prompting her to do and, in spite of urgings by the moderator, she did not say. In addition, a Jamaican respondent was reluctant to make comparisons between standard of living of the deaf in Jamaica and the United States but provided the information after he was encouraged to do so. The moderator also restricted some members in each group who tended to dominate the discussions while others were finding it difficult to make their comments.

Data Analysis

This study used the Constant Comparison Technique, discussed by Glaser and Straus (1967), Lincoln and Guba (1985), and Nicotera (1993) to combine explicit coding of qualitative data into quantitative categories and theoretic development from qualitative data. Glaser and Strauss explain that the Constant Comparison Method is designed to "aid the analyst...in generating a theory that is integrated, consistent, plausible, close to the data -- and at the same time is in a form clear enough to be readily ... operationalized for testing in quantitative research" (p. 103). The researcher in discussion with members of her academic committee selected this method of data analysis for its appropriateness in deriving grounded theory (Nicotera, 1993). The methodology allowed the researcher to make comparisons of findings for: 1) both Jamaican groups; 2) the African American group with the Jamaican groups; 3) the White American group with the African Americans; 4) the Jamaicans with the White Americans, and 5) all four groups. Through this process of comparison, the researcher was able to identify links between culture, stigma and deafness, as well as constitutive and regulative rules that the interactants use to deal with stigma.

The data for all four groups were audio taped, and the researcher transcribed and stored them in a file. When the analysis was to be done, the researcher collected index cards and made four stacks representing each group. The data were collected and the researcher identified units in accordance with the Constant Comparison Method. A unit is a set of information which not only serves "as the basis for defining categories" (Lincoln and Guba, 1985 p. 344) but "should have two characteristics. First it should be heuristic, that is, aimed at some understanding or some action that the inquirer needs to have to take. ... Second, it must be the smallest piece of information about something that can stand by itself, that is, it must be interpretable in the absence of any additional information other than a broad understanding of the context in which the inquiry is carried out" (p. 345). In analyzing the data, the researcher identified units of information in (a) the first Jamaican group; (b) the second Jamaican group; (c) the African American group; and (d) the white American group. Following are examples of units of information derived from the present study:

Jamaican Group A

1) "I feel good about myself." 2) "I feel normal." 3) "I feel good about myself when I am with deaf friends and family." 4) "Hearing people should stop the trouble and learn sign language." 5) "Hearing people should learn sign language." 6) "Hearing people should become more involved with deaf people." 7) "Sometimes they don't talk to me anymore and I don't know why." 8) "Sometimes I don't know what to do." 9) "I only communicate with people who are important for me to communicate with." 10) "I am happy with deaf people." 11) "The hearing people always start the trouble." 12) "The deaf do not trouble them."

Jamaican Group B

1) "I feel good about myself because I can control myself." 2) "When we have to communicate with hearing people who don't sign we use gestures." 3) "They say, don't show you (your) hand. Don't point. I feel hurt." 4) "They think because I am deaf I do bad things like stealing." 5) "I feel like fighting them." 6) "I ignore them." 7) "Hearing people need to learn sign language." 8) "If they laugh at me, I reason with them." 9) "Well some of the hearing people whisper dirty things about us, and so we do it, too." 10) "Hearing people are stupid." 11) "We laugh and call them fools." 12) "People have no understanding of us."

African American Group

1) "White people have a tendency to give us a lot of negative vibes." 2) "We try to encourage people to have positive attitudes that deaf people can..." 3) "We try to ignore a lot of this negative attitude [from white deaf]."" 4) "You feel like you're not welcome." 5) "I get on with deaf people." 6) "I feel a part of the deaf culture but there are so many differences..." 7) "They [hearing people] want to do the thinking for you." 8) "Hearing people need to understand deaf culture." 9) "They can treat us right." 10) "I feel good about myself." 11) "Hearing people need to understand deaf communication."

White American Group

1) "Hearing people ask dumb questions." 2) "They are less educated so they don't know much." 3) "I'm really proud of being deaf." 4) "... deaf people

know things in a different way." 5) "We are different." 6) " feel deaf first, but sometimes it depends on the environment." 7) "Black people are angry." 8) "Blacks don't volunteer." 9) "They [African American deaf] are kinda asking for it." 10) "Some white hearing people ignore us completely." 11) "I don't have the time to do that [explain deaf culture to hearing people.]"

The researcher identified 103 units of information in the first Jamaican group; 120 units for the second Jamaican group; 86 units for the African American group; and 93 for the white American group. Each unit was then entered on an index card. Each interactant in each group was then assigned a number which was written beside the unit of information on each card. Thus in the first Jamaican group, number 1 represented the first informant, and this number 1 was written beside each unit of information contributed by the first informant. This procedure was followed in the other three groups.

The units of information were then categorized according to the themes which had emerged. These themes were numbered 1-5: 1) definition of stigma and culture; 2) behaviors within the context of the deaf culture; 3) personal communication world view choices; 4) behaviors within either a working class or interethnic context; and 5) behaviors within either the low/high context culture. This was done separately for all four groups, and was the only logic by which the data were organized. The researcher felt that: 1) the questions posed lacked moderator bias as they had been discussed with the Academic Committee, and 2) such logical categories had been provided by the interactants themselves. A graduate student of Howard University who helped in categorizing the data confirmed the appropriateness of the themes. The five themes, then, emerged through the process of conducting the focus group and were confirmed by the constant comparison of the cards.

In addition to being assigned an interactant number beside the unit of information on each card, each informant was then assigned numbers indicating the themes reflecting the unit of information. Thus where informant number 1 expressed a unit of information reflective of theme number 3, the researcher developed a code 1-3. Where informant number 2 expressed a unit of information reflective of theme 5, the code was 2-5. This was done for all the informants in the first Jamaican group, the second Jamaican group, the African American group, and the white American group.

Category Properties

The next step was to "bring together into provisional categories those cards that apparently relate to the same content," (Lincoln and Guba, 1985, p. 347).

At this stage the cards were haphazardly arranged for each group and the researcher categorized them according to the criterion of "look/feel alike" (p.347). The categories reflected the five themes. In the process of categorization, "the first card represents the first entry in the first yet-to-be-named category" (p.347). " The second card is compared to the first and either placed with it or starts a new category. Each successive card is then placed in existing categories or used to start a new one" (Nicotera, 1993 p. 293). This method of data analysis required that cards which did not fit the categories were to be kept aside for later review. Each category was then titled with propositional statements to characterize each group of cards (Glaser and Strauss, 1967; Lincoln and Guba, 1985). The propositional statements which reflected the themes were as follows: 1) Definition of terms; 2) Behaviors as members of the deaf culture; 3) Individual Choices; 4) Behaviors as members of the working class; and 5) Behaviors as members of a high/low context culture. When the researcher needed to place a new card in an existing category, it was "included or excluded not on the basis of its look/feel alike quality, but on the basis of its fit-to-the rule" (Lincoln and Guba, p.448). Lincoln and Guba advise that unresolved cards in excess of 5-7% might represent a serious deficiency in the category set (p. 349). Two cards which contained information on "religion and deafness" and "women and deafness" and which emerged from the data in the White American group had been kept aside. Later they were reviewed and categorized with the cards dealing with behaviors within the context of the deaf culture. In the present study, each card for each of the groups was resolved. The researcher suggests that resolution arose from the relationship between the questions posed, the themes identified and the category properties developed.

Functionalist Canons

The present study rejects the functionalist paradigm which seeks to establish internal validity, external validity, reliability and objectivity in its method of inquiry. Internal validity is "the extent to which variations in an outcome (dependent) variable can be attributed to controlled variation in an independent variable. A causal connection between independent and dependent variables is usually assumed" (Lincoln and Guba 1985, p. 290). External validity, according to Cook and Campbell (1979), "is the approximate validity with which we infer that the presumed causal relationship can be generalized to and across alternate measures of the cause and effect, and across different types of persons, settings, and times" (p. 37). Ford (1975) describes reliability as occurring where "each repetition of the application of the same, or supposedly equivalent, instruments to the same units will yield similar measurements" (p.324). Finally, objectivity is defined as using methods "that by their character render the study beyond contamination by human foibles. Such a methodology is the experiment" (Lincoln and Guba, 1985 p. 292-293).

This study contends that these canons are inappropriate for this naturalistic inquiry. First, in relation to internal validity, it disputes the functionalist suggestion of an isomorphistic relationship between deafness as causality and stigma as effect. This relationship derives from an epistemological orientation which seeks to predict and control behavior, allowing Goffman to determine that the condition of deafness inevitably results in stigmatizing attitudes. However, this study posits that, from a naturalistic perspective, deaf individuals who belong to a deaf culture may not necessarily view deafness as a stigmatizing condition as "human behavior may exhibit a great deal of recurrent regularity that cannot be ascribed to causes ... [and therefore] to select one or a subset of ... factors as the cause or causes of some particular human behavior is fatuous" (Lincoln and Guba, 1985 p. 143).

Instead of focussing on causality, this study seeks to **understand** the pattern of relationships that exist between deafness, culture and stigma, and how individuals who are deaf **manage** stigma in different cultural situations. Thus, Lincoln and Guba suggest that "understanding involves the making of plausible imputations that depend on one's purpose. Out of the complex of mutually interactive shapers one may select those that afford some meaningful perspective in relation to the purpose that the investigator has in mind" (p.152). Management, on the other hand, enables the deaf to "provide the minimal elements needed for change or adaptation ... [while at the same time] ... block[ing] ... the most obvious constraining forces. The issue of what those minimal enabling elements and those most obvious constraining forces are can be resolved only by ... human intervention... [as] ... the focus of change is in the ...person affected..." (p.153). This study therefore suggests that there is no linear relationship between deafness and stigma but an interaction of deaf and hearing individuals in varied cultural contexts in which mutual simultaneous shaping of perceptions of deafness produce different behaviors which Goffman nomothetically describes as negative affect.

Nomic Generalization

Second, this study de-emphasizes the functionalist criterion of generalization which, from the paradigmatic perspective of the naturalist, is neither "warranted nor particularly desirable" (Lindlof 1995, p.238). According to Lincoln and Guba (1985), "there exists no consistent set of statements ... that can ever hope to deal with all propositions; some propositions will inevitably fall outside its purview..." (p. 118). This study suggests that the multiple constructed realities of deaf cultures do not have a fixed existence but are constantly changing. Therefore an investigator cannot identify universal laws which govern these relationships. Further, not only can generalizations be made only when specific conditions are met, but "they are [essentially] active creations of the mind. Empirically, they rest upon the generalizer's experience with a limited number of particulars ..." (Lincoln and Guba, 1985 p. 113).

Instead of seeking generalizable laws, this study suggests working hypotheses as the specific context of each culture makes it difficult, if not impossible, to predict that deaf individuals in other cultures will respond to stigmatizing behavior in similar ways. Cronbach (1975) reminds that, "...when we give proper weight to local conditions, any generalization is a working hypothesis, not a conclusion" (pp. 124-125).

The Role of Values

Third, functionalism claims a 'value-free' method of inquiry rendering research objective and uncontaminated by assumptions, perspectives and norms. But the literature suggests four sources of value which impact research and which values may either be in resonance or dissonance with each other: "... the values of the investigator personally, the values undergirding the substantive paradigm that guides the inquiry, the values undergirding the methodological paradigm that guides the inquiry, and the values that inhere in the cultural setting within which the inquiry is carried out" (Lincoln and Guba, 1985 p. 174). In addition, these researchers advise that the functionalist "runs the risk of overlooking other possible perspectives and, therefore, of being fair to differing points of view. If objectivity is a useful criterion, fairness is even more so" (p.173).

This study makes no claim to a value free inquiry but recognizes that it is value-bound. It admits the inherent naturalistic stance of ideological openness rather than a functionalist's ideological blatantness "of using ideology to serve one's own ends... one has no choice about representing some ideology -- one cannot be alive without one. The real issue is whether one consciously takes account of it or if it is left to guide one's own judgement" (Lincoln and Guba, 1985 p. 185). The present researcher has been interacting with members of the deaf culture for three years, but this interaction has **influenced** rather than **shaped** her perceptions of how members of the deaf culture manage stigma. Thus this study seeks to understand the role that culture plays in the de-stigmatization process. Finally, this study suggests the invalidity of reliability.

It contends that the flexible and unpredictable nature of human behavior defies "measurement" and therefore can not be accurately observed, replicated, predicted or controlled.

Standards of Credibility, Dependability and Confirmability

The present study proposes the standards of credibility, dependability, and confirmability developed by Lincoln and Guba (1985) as alternatives to the functionalist criteria for research. These researchers suggest that credibility will likely increase when the investigator spends time with the interactants to learn their culture, to test for misinformation introduced by distortion, and also to build trust. For three years, the present researcher interacted with members of the deaf culture at Gallaudet University, seeking to gain insights into the culture and later to learn the techniques of closed captioning for television programs. However, in relation to the Jamaican deaf culture, the researcher did not have extended interaction with its members but found it relatively easy to interact with these informants as she herself is of Jamaican nationality. To reduce misinformation in the focus groups, the investigator ensured that each group had an interpreter who represented at least one of their cultures. Thus, the Jamaicans had a Jamaican interpreter; the African Americans had an African American interpreter; and the white Americans had a white American interpreter. Also, in each case, the interpreter had been working in the particular deaf culture for many years. Informants were therefore able to clarify and explain their information. In relation to the necessity for building trust, the researcher explained to the informants that, while the research would contribute to scholarship requirements, she also hoped to work with the Jamaican deaf culture in the area of research and closed captions for television. The respondents in each culture were very supportive, and an African American summarized:

> ... you have come here to learn about deaf culture. You are motivated. I would like to see hearing people try to be the same.

The knowledge gained about the deaf culture in the years of interacting with its members at Gallaudet and sharing the nationality of the Jamaicans and race of the African Americans did not enable the researcher to "go native ... and become so like the group ... that she ceased to consider either her cultural or professional subgroup as her dominant reference group ... and begins a 'performance - understanding' role within the studied group" (Lincoln and Guba, 1985 p. 303). Apart from the fact that this researcher had no intention of "going native" there were objective constraints. First she was not fluent in either American or Jamaican Sign Languages and this restricted any merger. Second, sharing the race of African Americans did not facilitate entry to their deaf culture. She was a hearing person and viewed to be on the outside of the deaf culture. One informant said:

You have come here to learn about deaf culture ...

Third, being a Jamaican was not a pre-requisite for understanding the Jamaican deaf culture and, in one focus group discussion, the researcher's credibility was questioned by one informant:

What would you do with **your** child if he were deaf?

Investigator: "I would learn to sign and send my child to a deaf school." The investigator also did member checks to ensure the credibility of the information. "Member checks are opportunities for the researcher to test hypotheses, concepts, interpretations, or explanations with members of the local culture he or she is studying" (Lindlof, 1995 p. 240). With respect to the Jamaicans, the checks were done with the principal at the school who knew the students enough to confirm that the information they gave was credible. She also said that other deaf individuals who did not share similar home and school environment might have reported differently.

Member checks were also done with staff members of Gallaudet University. They verified the information given by both African American and White American groups and prior to the focus group discussions advised that each group have an interpreter of its own race to provide a "comfort level" among the interactants. Also, the naturalist focusses on transferability instead of the functionalist's criterion of external validity, and thus the study presents the data unedited, rich, and as emerged in the discussions. Scholars and subsequent researchers may be able to decide if this information can be applied to other contexts.

Dependability was ensured as the investigator worked very closely with her principal advisor, Dr. William Starosta, and the other members of her Academic Committee. The committee met when required, discussed the progress of the research, and made recommendations. With reference to confirmability of the data, the researcher kept notes, tapes and transcripts of the discussions. However, in accordance with the regulation of the

Institutional review Board at Gallaudet and Howard Universities, the information was destroyed on the completion of the project.

The researcher now discusses the research findings.

Chapter 5

Research Findings

In this chapter the researcher first reports the discussions and then presents the findings derived from the process of constant comparison.

JAMAICAN GROUP 1
(1) Definition of stigma and culture

None of the Jamaican informants knew the word "stigma." The researcher provided Goffman's definition and they all reported that the term they use for their experience of stigma is "trouble." They also indicated that they are 'troubled' mostly by hearing adults.

Rose: "We don't know stigma but we know trouble. That is what hearing people do to us. They trouble us when they tease us...when they laugh at us ... when they call us 'dummy'... and they don't want to be with us or play with us. That is trouble."

Jane: "We call it trouble. They [persons who are hearing] trouble you [us]."

Jill: "People trouble me a lot and call me stupid."

Brad: "...Hearing people in America are not very nice. They trouble deaf people like the hearing people in Jamaica trouble us..."

Olga: "It is difficult to tell about their body movements, but we can tell when they are using body movements to trouble us. I read their body movements."

Also, none of the subjects understood the term "deaf culture" but reported that deaf people in Jamaica are like "family."

Jim: "I don't understand culture. You mean what?

Sally: "You mean if we are close like family? ...we are...deaf people all good friends. We play games, go to Coney Park, gossip. We also go to the movies. Sometimes we do not hear what is going on at the movies but we feel the vibration and we try to read lips. We love the movies. We also go skating..."

Olga: "We do plenty things together...even being here at Lister Mair is a good thing for deaf people. I didn't believe in deaf school before, but I am happy to be in deaf school with deaf children. They teach me to use sign language and I feel good about myself."

Brad: "I went to America with my mother and uncle to live, and I was happy with the deaf people. We had our own bus. We never had to pay for lunch. I am happy with deaf people here but I have to pay for lunch and food."

Jane: "...I feel comfortable among my deaf friends..."

Olga: "Yeah..." "We do the same things like other deaf people. ...even in America. We use the book 'The Joy of Signing' that other deaf people in other places use. Deaf people do a lot of good things...like Miss America...she is deaf. She is one of us and we are proud." (Applause from the entire group).

Jim: "Yeah, yeah..."

(2) Behaviors within the context of the Deaf Culture

To identify some of their behaviors within the context of the deaf culture, the researcher asked them how they felt about deafness and how this perception affected their response to 'trouble.' Four of the students said that it was okay to be deaf; four were disappointed but only because hearing people gave them 'trouble'; and one refused to talk about it. However, all nine applauded a comment that it was okay to be deaf when they had friends and family who loved and understood them. All nine students reported that they deliberately selected the hearing persons with whom they wanted to communicate, that they were willing to facilitate communication with hearing people, but that hearing people should learn sign language.

Sally: "I feel okay ... very okay. I do not feel worried. I feel normal."

Jane: "I feel disappointed because when hearing people find out I am deaf, they call me dummy."

Olga: "When I am with hearing people I feel sad when they laugh and call me dummy."

Brad: "I feel good about myself. I feel some hearing people are stupid... sometimes we laugh at them when they think we are stupid because they are stupid to think we are stupid."

June: "Yeah, I was born deaf, but when I was in school at Hope Road I didn't think I was deaf. I didn't think I was hearing. I didn't think anything about myself. I felt normal. I was four years old. When I became six years old, that was when I find out. My teacher told me at the deaf school. All the children ...the children used sign language and I used sign language too. Being deaf doesn't mean anything...only when people tease me."

Edna: "I don't want to talk about it [deafness]...nobody discuss it with me before ... my family don't talk to me about it." (She started to cry).

Jill: "I feel bad about deafness ... when I was six years old and I went to Portmore to live with my mother; she took me to school to learn about my future... In the evening when I was six years old, I had to go home by myself. I didn't know where I lived and sometimes I got lost, but people helped me. My mother did not come for me at school. I got lost. ... She had problems, maybe...maybe she was ashamed of me. I feel bad."

Sally: "When I was in hearing school I was the only one who was deaf. The hearing children do not love me. I feel so sad that no-one loved me...only one child...one girl. The teacher punished me a lot because I didn't speak in school. I was afraid and I shut my mouth even tighter. I always told my mother that the teacher always punish me and my mother went to school and told her I was deaf. She was in shock. She said she didn't know that I was deaf. My family took me away from the school and sent me to deaf school...I feel good about myself. It is okay to be deaf especially when we have deaf friends and family who love us. They understand me and I understand them " (Applause from every group member).

Jim: "I feel good with my deaf friends... but I feel ... I want to talk. I want to talk to hearing people. People are embarrassed around me. Others tease me..."

Question: "How do you communicate with hearing people?"

Edna: "I communicate with people who are deaf. Not much hearing. Only my mother and my father."

Jim: "By writing and teaching them sign language... by using gestures ... making signs...writing a lot. Sometimes my brother tries to sign, and I help him by teaching him."

June: "I don't communicate a lot with hearing people. Only those that I must. Like my grandmother."

Sally: "I only communicate with people who are important for me to communicate with, because it is difficult. Many hearing people don't use sign language and when I write, they say they don't understand the words... sometimes they talk to me and I look at their lips and try to understand... sometimes I ask them to slow down... sometimes they walk away.."

Brad: "Hearing people should try and communicate with deaf people. They should learn to sign..."

Jim: "All policemen and doctors. Everybody should learn sign. When I write, they don't understand and it is difficult for me. If they learn sign language, they would be able to explain a lot of things and I would understand a lot of things." (Applause).

(3) Personal Communication World View Choices

The informants also discussed some personal choices they make in communicating with the hearing:

The responses ranged from passive to active. Two engaged in physical confrontation; one was determined to prove her worth; two withdrew from confrontation and one opted to stay indoors often.

Brad: "Some hearing children fight with me and give me trouble ... and I fight back. ... I fight with a hearing boy in America once when he was troubling me.."

Olga: "I don't like to go out a lot..."

Jane: "Sometimes the trouble gets too much for me and I fight them. I quarrel with them. The hearing should not do this to us. But then after I fight a little, I just stop and I ignore them."

Rose: "I feel like fighting them sometimes, but then I don't bother."

Jim: "I want to play football, and although I can play, when the hearing people find out I am deaf, they tell me that I cannot play and I ... leave."

Sally: "When I was ten years old, I couldn't ride my bicycle. So my hearing friends laughed and said 'You can't ride bicycle' One day I tried and tried. I fall off, but I tried again. When I could ride, I told my friends that I could ride, and they said 'let's see. And when they saw me riding, everyone was surprised."

(4) Behaviors within the working class context

The informants discussed their behavior within the working class culture. Each responses indicated a respect for authority and a willingness to avoid confrontation. All the students agreed that the hearing culture generally apologizes for 'troubling' them.

Jane: "My father never communicates with me. He ignores me. I try ..."

Jim: "We ignore hearing people when they trouble us. We ignore them a lot."

Question: "Why?"

Response: "My teachers and my parents tell me to ignore them."

General Response in the group: "Yes, yes." "That's true."

Sally: "Sometimes we ignore them because they always start the trouble. The deaf do not trouble them."

Edna: "The hearing persons cannot look at a deaf person and know that the deaf person is deaf. Only when we try to talk and only when we have difficulty in communicating. Then they are surprised and open their mouths wide. Then they look like they are sorry for us being deaf. Sometimes they tell us that they are sorry. That happens a lot. Then they speak slowly after they find out."

(5) Behaviors within the high context culture

In discussing their behaviors in the high context culture, only six students responded and their responses indicated that they derive meaning from the context of the interaction.

Olga: "It depends on which hearing person I am communicating with. If they are my family and they know I am deaf, it is okay, because they already know. But when it is a stranger who is hearing, sometimes I don't know what to do ..."

Brad: "Sometimes they [hearing people] don't talk to me anymore, and I don't know why..."

Jane: "My father never communicates with me. He ignores me. I try...I think he doesn't understand me...maybe."

Jim: "A long time ago when I was in another school, the teacher used to beat me a lot...I don't know why."

June: "When people tease me...I wonder why..."

Jill: "My mother did not come for me at school. I got lost. ... maybe, maybe she was ashamed of me."

Sally: "I went home and asked my mother why I was deaf and she said that God made me that way. I said, 'No way!' Other people can talk!"

JAMAICAN GROUP 2
(1) Definition of stigma and culture

As was the case with group one, none of the informants in group two had ever met the word 'stigma.' They too used the word 'trouble.' They also reported that they are stigmatized mostly by hearing adults.

Steve: "I would like hearing people to stop the trouble. I would like them to stop calling me dummy. I would like them to leave me alone, but they always give me trouble."

John: "I want to buy a bread, and because the shopkeeper doesn't understand me, I have to point [to indicate what he wants] and he doesn't understand me, and then I point again and make gestures and he says: 'Come out a me shop an go on to yu yaad' [get out of my shop and go home] and then I leave without getting the bread. They say 'don't show your hand. Don't point.' That is trouble."

Craig: " ...sometimes people throw stones at me and hit me. That is big trouble."

Keba: "Hearing people give deaf people a lot of trouble. Sometimes I know when they are saying bad things about me because I watch their lips, and when they are done, I tell them to go away."

Sarah: "Sometimes hearing people give me a lot of trouble. The men talk bad and dirty to me ... they always talk about sex to me and make sexual gestures. The hearing men always say 'I love you' to me. I don't like that."

The subjects discussed their perceptions of deafness and of the deaf culture. Like group one, they did not know what 'deaf culture' meant, but all said that deaf people are friends.

(2) Behaviors within the context of the Deaf Culture

Eight informants reported positive attitudes towards themselves as being deaf. The attitudes were influenced by support from family; being friends with each other, sharing common interests, and identifying with achievements of deaf people. One informant reported a negative attitude towards deafness. Each reported that they choose which members of the hearing culture they want to communicate with. All indicated that they try to facilitate communication but they all reported that hearing people should learn to sign.

Sarah: "Deaf people do a lot of things together... go to the movies; even here at Lister Mair, we are friends..."

Greta: "Yeah, good friends and we laugh at hearing people ...

sometimes."

Grace: "Wait, let me talk about that!... Hearing people are stupid. I laugh when they speak to me in mumble jumble because they think I am stupid, that I don't understand. I laugh and they laugh because they think that I think that their mumble jumble is funny. But I laugh because they look stupid and they behave stupid" (Applause from every member of the group.)

John: "Hearing people usually mumble to deaf people and then say: 'Do you understand?' They tease us when they mumble. Then we laugh and call them fools in sign language (applause). They do not know that we understand them."

Steve: "Nothing is wrong with deaf people. We have our friends and family and we feel good about ourselves. ... deaf people should always stick together."

Grace: "Some deaf people are famous ... like Miss America ...there are deaf dancers. Some deaf people win medals. Deaf people win speech competition in signing and travel around the world ..." (applause).

Max: "I think hearing people are stupid because when they don't want to play football with me, what does that have to do with anything? What does deafness have to do with kicking a ball? They are so stupid!"

Greta: "I feel good about myself because I can control myself. I can communicate with both deaf and hearing. I can handle myself on the road. My deafness is not a disability."

Craig: "I am sorry that I am deaf. I can't hear. I can't talk properly. People can't understand what I am saying... my parents don't deal with deafness. They don't sign. They can't communicate with me and I get angry."

John: "I sit down and watch hearing people talk, and they call me a thief, and I say, 'No. I am not a thief.' They think because I am deaf, I do bad things, like stealing. They are liars and I don't think highly of them. Deaf people are better off with each other."

Joy: "Hearing people are good, but they need to learn sign language, so that they can communicate with us and understand us. Doctors, policemen especially." (applause from each group member).

Keba: "I want hearing people to learn sign language and I will teach anyone who wants to learn. They must learn to respect deaf people..."

Grace: "I communicate with some hearing and some deaf. But mainly I communicate with hearing people who are my teachers and my family. It is difficult to use gestures because hearing people don't understand... I still try."

John: "I communicate only with my hearing family, my teachers and some people at the Seventh Day Adventist Church. Sometimes we meet hearing people on the bus and, when they see us sign, they ask us if we are deaf and we tell them. We try to use gestures and write notes to them but they still don't understand. It is difficult to communicate with some hearing people."

Keba: "Sometimes we meet hearing people who sign and we communicate with them. But its hard to manage because hearing people have no understanding of us. If they learnt sign language it would be better. All society should learn sign language" (applause).

(3) Personal Communication World View Choices

The respondents discussed the personal choices they make in communicating with the hearing:

The responses included fighting, reasoning, and avoiding.

John: "...They say, 'Don't show your hand.' 'Don't point.' I feel hurt so I don't ask them for [what I want] again."

Sarah: "One hearing man in a shop started speaking dirty to me and made sexual gestures. I signed to him that, if he continued, I was going to punch him. I quarreled with him and I quarrel with them all the time when they pinch me on my bottom and when they speak dirty to me. I fight. They must not do that. They must respect me. They take advantage of me because I am deaf, but I will not let them do that. I fight back."

Max: "When they give me trouble, I curse them..."

Greta: "Well, I fight them, because, if they fight me, what am I supposed to do? My mother says 'If they trouble you, thump them!'"

Grace: "If they laugh at me, I reason with them ..."

Sarah: "...I curse them and tell my father and my father defends me."

Joy: "Sometimes I stay indoors and do not do much interacting..."

Max: "When they think I am stupid, I write what I want to say and I act out what I mean. I am not stupid, then they say 'Hey you can do everything!'"

(4) Behaviors within the Working Class Context

The groups also discussed their behaviors within a working class context.

They all reported that parents, teachers and other members of the hearing community tell them to ignore 'trouble.' Also, they reported that hearing persons always apologized for giving them 'trouble.'

Joy: "If hearing people trouble me, I can't be bothered. I just ignore them and leave. Sometimes when the men talk to me about sex, it hurts me, but I just ignore them."

Steve: "I am innocent, they are guilty so I ignore them. It is better to leave hearing people alone when they give us trouble because it causes too much trouble when we fight."

Joy: "When they give me trouble I ignore them. Sometimes hearing people tell us to ignore them ... parents sometimes ... sometimes teachers and people at the church. They tell us it is better not to fight" (The group agrees and subjects nod).

Keba: "Hearing people call us dummy a lot. And I tell them that they are feisty and then they say they are sorry that they call us dumb. They always come back and say they are sorry ..."

Group members: "Yes ... yeah."

John: "They always say they are sorry but when the tell me they are sorry it is too late because I feel bad already." (applause).

(5) Behaviors within the High Context Culture

Five informants then responded to questions relating to their high context culture.

Three of them said that they do not understand why hearing people 'trouble' them; two seek to know by asking direct questions.

Joy: "Sometimes when they give me trouble, I ask them why and they just walk away. I don't know why they do these things ..."

Greta: "Sometimes I know why they do it. Sometimes I don't. It depends. When hearing men talk to me about sex, I don't know if they are troubling me because I am deaf or because I am a girl ... I think about it sometimes."

Keba: "I understand sometimes. When I try to write and use gestures and they walk away, I know it is because I am deaf. But sometimes some of the hearing people try to understand me and then I don't understand why hearing people cannot try to understand me all the time."

Steve: "I do not understand why when they find out that I am deaf they don't want to play football with me anymore ... it does not make sense to me ..."

Grace: "If they laugh at me, I reason with them. I ask them why they laugh and they say they think I am stupid ... I understand why."

DISCUSSIONS WITH THE AFRICAN AMERICAN GROUP
(1) Definition of stigma and culture

The researcher asked them to define 'stigma.' None of the subjects knew what it meant. The researcher provided Goffman's definition and they all reported that they are stigmatized by hearing people but moreso by Deaf Whites. They agreed that they share the following experiences.

Carl: "It's funny when you sit back and watch hearing people. They want to do the thinking for you, or assume that you don't know ..."

Dave: "When I was growing up, hearing people would make fun of the way we signed. They mocked us ... made fun of us. That happened many times. Like I didn't fit in the scheme of things ..."

With respect to their understanding of the term 'deaf culture' and their relationship to the culture, each respondent said that, although they were deaf, they did not consider themselves to be totally integrated in the Deaf culture. They all report choosing to interact with individuals who are deaf and not wanting to make effort to facilitate communication with the hearing. Only one informant reported attempting to facilitate communication with the hearing.

Kimal: "I was raised in it, but I feel like kind of half and half..." (Group members nod in agreement).

Carl: "I was raised up at Kendall [school for the deaf], I went to MSSD [school for the deaf] and then here at Gallaudet. I get on with deaf people...but with white deaf people, they involve themselves with you for a short period of time ... with Black deaf people I think we are like family..." (group members nod in agreement).

Sandra: "I feel a part of the deaf culture but there are so many differences to deal with ... those who are from hearing families etc. So how can you really define deaf culture when there are so many different groups? I know I am deaf, but I don't really know if I am in the culture or not."

Kimal: "I am from a mainstream school in Ohio ... they [white deaf] will come up and ask, 'Are you from a mainstream institute or a deaf institute?' And I say, 'I'm from mainstream school' and then I never hear from them again. They trying to say you don't have enough deaf culture in you. I don't believe in that. I believe that if you have a hearing problem and you want to learn about deaf culture, you have a right ..."

(2) Behavior within the Context of the Deaf Culture

Kimal: "I do not feel like deafness is a disability. I don't. I couldn't create myself. God did, and I am special. We are like everyone."

Wayne: "It is not a disability because we can do everything that hearing people can do. We just can't hear, that's all. So I don't think it's the same as a disability ..."

Bev: "Many deaf people can do anything. God made me special."

Sandra: "There were times when I used to hide my deafness. I would try to talk, to communicate with hearing people. Being at Gallaudet has helped me to accept my culture."

Dave: "I couldn't accept myself as deaf, but now I have to. I am going to be deaf forever."

Carl: "Sometimes I wish that I could talk."

Sandra: "I have some hearing friends and, when I was young, I felt that hearing people had no patience because when they explained something and it wasn't clear, when I asked them, they would go 'Oh God, I will tell you later.' ... after a while, I just didn't want to interact with that kind of hearing person, so that is when I started to communicate more with deaf peoples cause you could communicate more openly and freely. And sometimes it is hard to communicate with hearing people cause they are always in a rush. And it takes time for things to get interpreted ... I communicate with my hearing family, they support me in that they think deaf people can do anything."

Kimal: "... I tend to interact with deaf people because its easier in the interaction..."

Group members: "Yeah, yeah."

Bev: "Many times I am going out and I try to communicate by speaking. Sometimes I really don't understand what they [the hearing] are saying and I try to answer them. I try to read their lips ..."

Wayne: "Now sometimes I think hearing people do not have a lot of patience because they cannot understand deaf communication, and sometimes they think it is taking too much time. If they don't have the patience then they leave. I don't stop them."

Dave: "... I don't waste time with them ..."

Sandra: "For example in the library, someone came up and asked me a question and, when he found out I was deaf, he just turned away and left. It didn't bother me."

Carl: "Sometimes they offend me, but once they play dumb with me, I play dumb with them too."

Kimal: "... Giving [getting] too much expression [from hearing persons] bothers me, and then I get an attitude. But, if it looks like they really want to do something, then I can reciprocate. If they want to give up and have a bad attitude, I just leave it. That's their way."

Carl: "Hearing people should learn about deaf culture. There are books at the book store, they can read. For example, you have come here to learn about deaf culture. You are motivated. I would like to see other hearing people do the same."

Kimal: "They should learn to respect us" (applause).

(3) Personal Communication World View Choices

With respect to their personal choices in communicating, they all reported that it depended on whether they were communicating with the hearing or communicating with the white deaf. In communicating with the former they all indicate that they "fight for equality."

One respondent said that he sometimes engaged in physical confrontation.

Wayne: "Hearing people don't think we are equal so we fight."

Question: How do you fight?

Sandra: "By approaching people directly and telling them what we want." (They all nod in agreement).

Wayne: "Like my sister ... she yelled at me: 'I wish my brother wasn't deaf. He's so stupid.' And I said: 'Go ahead, insult me, it doesn't bother me. I'm your brother. You're my sister and you have to accept the way your brother is. Period. That's all you've got. That's all I've got.' "

Kimal: "Well back in high school I used to fight. Physical fight. I had to fight all the time ..."

(4) Behaviors Within an Interethnic Context

They all reported that they face the most stigmatizing attitudes from White Americans who are deaf.

Kimal: "We try our best to say we can do it [to resist stigmatizing attitudes] ... we try to ignore a lot of their negative attitude ... we try to fight for what we want, but you have to fight for so many things ... and sometimes it seems as if you are never going to succeed."

The respondents discussed their responses to stigmatizing attitudes within an interracial context.

Sandra: "Within our [deaf culture] we are discriminated against..."

Kimal: "Growing up as a deaf person I never faced much problem. It wasn't until I came to Gallaudet that I saw the separation because I was really surprised about this deaf culture thing and the differences, the different perspectives. White deaf people have a tendency to give us a lot of negative vibes and we try to encourage people to have positive attitudes that Black deaf people can, but white deaf people don't seem to think that way. ... Like they feel like Black deaf people can't participate in the student body government and in other organizations. They kinda give a lot of excuses as to why you can't get in the program ... 'you're not deaf enough' ... and they try to set up some type of oppressive reason why Black deaf people can't get into the organizations."

Carl: "You feel like you're not welcome. You feel like you're not getting the kinds of services that you need. We wanted an African American course here. So far, you have a Spanish Literature; you have a French literature; and you have German literature. But we don't have any African American literature course, and we wanted to see that added. We wanted a Black history course added here. And so we face that problem. We do have an organization of Black deaf students and we come together to express our problem. ... like we send letters to the administration about our concerns. We try and do those things..."

Kimal: "... Mainstream school was pretty tough. I had to grow up real quick. I had to think of living. Living to see the next day. It was tough. But when I came here, it was a different story. It was like, I knew about racism, but at home (Ohio) they don't flaunt you with it. They try you here at Gallaudet ... This is strange ... it's like white deaf people here at Gallaudet can accept gays and lesbians, but they can't accept you being black and deaf. I don't get it."

Sandra: "I'm from New York City, and I went to a deaf school. The first time I came to Gallaudet, I had a white room mate ... During the first semester, she wanted me to move so she could have a new [white] room mate. She said she couldn't move because she had back problems, and I said, 'well, I've got back problems too.' To survive the situation, I went ahead and moved out ..."

Dave: "I don't feel like I am getting any positive support from whites here. It's always very negative ..."

Wayne: "We just deal with this racism. ...we are used to it ...we don't let it interrupt our lives. We just kinda go on with our lives."

Bev: "Yeah."

(5) Behaviors Within a Low Context Culture

One respondent summed up their general behavior towards hearing persons within a low context culture: "... I say to them: 'look, tell me what was being said. Tell me what was going on.' "

The respondents agreed that they generally ask the hearing person to explain the behavior if the message was not clear.

DISCUSSIONS WITH WHITE AMERICAN GROUP
(1) Definition of Stigma and Culture

None of these informants knew the word 'stigma.' The researcher provided Goffman's definition.

They all reported that they are stigmatized mostly by "the young. The whites. High school students. Junior High school students..**Junior high!**..."

Helen: "They [hearing people] ask dumb questions like 'Do you drive?' Of course we drive. They always confuse hearing with visual impairment. Or they discount us, you know. For example, one time I was with my sister to go roller skating (my sister is hearing) and her hearing friends made fun of us signing."

Suzie: "They look down at you. They stare at you. You know, quite in your face. They invade our privacy or they'll ask stupid questions like, 'Can you dance?' ' Can you read?' Those kinds of things ..."

They all knew what culture meant. They said they identified with and were proud to be part of the Deaf culture.

Vickie: "I'm really proud of being deaf. My family is deaf. We are very close to other deaf people. We are white, but we consider ourselves deaf first..."

Barbara: "To me, they are equally important. But look at me. I am woman, and I am White. You would probably see me as a White woman first, and then deaf. But when we go into the hearing world, I feel deaf first."

Fay: "Deaf first ... I look at hearing people and say they don't **have** anything. They don't **know** how we feel. So I feel proud of myself and all of us are from deaf families. So we have much better self-esteem, I think..."

Fay: "Deaf ... Sometimes I think deaf people know things in a different way. Hearing people just hear sounds, but deaf people see things in a different way. That way we learn more."

Burke: "I'm deaf first and white after. ... I'm proud to be deaf ...Yeah, yeah it's true. Maybe this will mess up your research study [laughter]."

Helen: "I feel deaf first, but sometimes it depends on the environment. For example, if I am around a bunch of Catholic people, then I feel Jewish first."

(2) Behaviors Within the Context of the Deaf Culture

They all agreed that they confront stigmatizing behaviors.

Helen: "We just like ... to the question, 'Do you drive?' We say 'yes, of course. We can see the road ...' "

Suzie: "If people make fun of me for signing, then I make my mouth movement imitating them and make fun of them back."

Barbara: "I feel sorry for these people. They are ignorant."

Common response: "Yeah, Yeah."

Fay: "These people are less educated so they don't know much..."

Common response: "True ... true."

They all indicate that as they are proud of their culture they do not think it necessary to facilitate communication with the hearing. The latter should become involved with the culture if they want to learn about the deaf.

Burke: "We are different. We have our own values. We carry on a tradition."

Fay: "We can never become oralists in a hearing world. We are different and proud of who we are."

Barbara: "Some white hearing people are not very nice. Some are mean. Some are stupid. Same way with the Black hearing. Some white hearing people ignore us completely. Other hearing people (she mimics a patronizing tone) 'want to learn sign language so they can help us.' (laughter).

(3) Behaviors Within the Context of Their Personal Communication World View

They all reported that their personal interaction with the hearing was determined by their view of themselves as a culture. Hence they agreed with Fay. "They keep coming up and asking us 'How do you sign this? How do you sign that? Well excuse me, but I just don't have the time to do that! I'm sorry! If they want to learn about the deaf, get involved with the culture!"

However, Vickie remarked, "I feel angry ... sometimes I wish I could... They are just making fun of us for fun."

(4) Behaviors Within an Interethnic Context

Helen: "Well, I'm from California and, where I come from, race doesn't seem to bother us. Black, Hispanic, white, oriental, it doesn't matter. But here at Gallaudet, I can see big separations between the Blacks and the Whites, and maybe that's affecting their perspective on White Deaf people. Probably Washington DC is having an effect on Gallaudet."

Vickie: "I'm from Maryland myself and I think D.C. does have an effect on Gallaudet. Sometimes I feel people misinterpret what I say or sign..."

Burke: "It doesn't have anything to do with deafness, because we are [Black and White] both deaf. It has to do with race and attitude. That's really obvious here. It doesn't have anything to do with deafness." (They nod agreement).

Barbara: "I think its crazy. For example, SBG (he's a member by the way). The SBG is open to volunteers, but who comes to volunteer? Most of the time they, the Blacks, don't volunteer. So in a way they're kinda asking for it."

Burke: "Sometimes we have interviews for positions on the SBG and a number of the Black students here ... there are not really that many, compared to whites. The competition is high, so I can only pick one person, and I pick the best person and most of the time he happens to be white ..."

Fay: "When Black deaf people say that they are not deaf enough to be part of the culture, I think that's just a racist attitude. They look at everything in terms of race. I don't understand what they are talking about. But maybe, here's some food for thought ... maybe they think of themselves as Black first and deaf after. And maybe that's the answer. We feel deaf first, and then white. Maybe that's the difference here at Gallaudet. So ... maybe that's why they feel that they don't have the same relationship with others here." (They nod in agreement).

(5) Behaviors Within a Low Context Culture

The group agreed with Helen's summary of their behavior within this context:

> We just like ... to the question, 'do you drive?' We say, 'Yes, of course. We can see the road.' If people make fun of me for signing, then I make my mouth movement imitating them and make fun of them back.

Constant Comparisons

The data confirm that responses to the perception that deafness is negatively different vary and that cultural differences among the three deaf cultures account for these variations.

Group Comparisons

With respect to similarities, 1) none of the groups interviewed had known of the word 'stigma'; 2) both the Jamaicans and the White Americans identified themselves as belonging to a deaf culture; 3) all of the groups described stigmatizers as "stupid"; 4) African Americans and White Americans within the low context culture both focussed on the message to determine stigmatizing behavior; and 5) each group reported a minority position that engaged in physical confrontation with stigmatizers or wished to express a behavior contrary to that required by the culture. There were also similarities in cultural rules. Both African Americans and Jamaicans chose to communicate with some members of the hearing community and ignore others.

Several differences existed among the groups. With the exception of the Jamaicans: 1) none had labeled their experience of stigma; 2) African Americans who are deaf regarded themselves as black first and deaf after; 3) each deaf culture had different expectations of the hearing. The Jamaicans expected the hearing to learn sign language; the African Americans expected the hearing to respect them; and the White Americans expected the hearing to learn about the deaf culture.

With respect to differences in cultural rules, Jamaicans reported communicating only with those hearing persons that which is "important and necessary"; African Americans advised communicating only with those who are willing to or who express a need to communicate with them; White Americans suggested that hearing persons learn the culture. Within the interethnic context, differences also exist. African Americans avoided stigmatizing behaviors of Whites, while Whites argued that the cultural differences existed because African Americans place primary importance on race, Whites emphasize deafness.

The researcher also found differences in the personal communication world view choices. Jamaicans said that they reason with the stigmatizers or avoid them. African Americans report that they fight for equality in their interaction with the hearing and avoid racist behaviors of the American Whites who are deaf. The White Americans who are deaf indicate that they do not think it is their responsibility to communicate with the hearing as they will never be "oralists in a hearing world."

Chapter 6

Inappropriateness of Goffman's Functionalist Analysis

Two research questions guided this study: 1) What links, if any, can be demonstrated among culture, deafness and stigma? 2) What are the constitutive and regulative rules that selected deaf populations use in dealing with stigmatization? In this chapter the researcher documents the claimed advantages of the study, discusses how the research questions have been answered, and makes recommendations for future research.

Goffman's theory of stigma derives from the positivist tradition which allows human as scientist to "develop a theory of truth" by "standing apart from the world and be [ing] able to experiment and theorize about it objectively and dispassionately" (Hess, 1980 p. vii). However "almost every assumption underlying this account has been subjected to damaging criticism" (Hess, 1980 p. vii). This study documents another criticism of a theoretical perspective derived from the positivist tradition.

In developing his theory, Goffman (1963) discusses " 'mixed contacts' -- the moments when stigmatized and normal are in the same 'social situation,' that is, in one another's immediate physical presence, whether in a conversation-like encounter or in the mere co-presence of an unfocussed gathering" (p.12). There is no focus on interaction; thus, the central feature of his analysis is the negative attribution to the "condition" (of difference) in mixed contacts, in the presence of the "normal;" and in "encounters." These categories -- "mixed contacts," presence of "normals," "encounters," and "co-presence" become the functionalist's "physical and therefore mechanical world" (Wolf, 1981, p.56) in which deaf persons exist.

Goffman places the deaf in a mechanistic world in which the social setting categorizes them as not "whole and usual person[s] ...[but] tainted [and] discounted..." (p.3). This categorization becomes a "logical law" within the functionalist tradition and similarly the issue of "acceptance" by "normals," which Goffman presents as the central feature of a deaf person's life, becomes another "logical law." These laws, which Goffman identifies as governing "mixed contacts" between deaf and hearing individuals, become, in the functionalist tradition, universal forces which determine that such contacts between deaf and hearing persons are predictable. Hess (1980) contends:

> ... there is an external world which can in principle be exhaustively described in scientific language. The scientist, as both observer and language user, can capture the external facts of the world in propositions that are true if they correspond to the facts and false if they do not. Science is ideally a linguistic system in which true propositions are in one-to-one relation to facts, including facts that are not directly observed because they involve hidden entities or properties, or past events or far distant events. These hidden events are described as theories, and theories can be inferred from observations, that is, the hidden explanatory mechanism of the world can be discovered from what is open to observation. (p.vii)

From his functionalist perspective, Goffman develops a theory of stigma which predicts that the deaf 1) feel unsure of how others will identify them, 2) do not know to which "category" they will be assigned, 3) do not know how they will be defined in the "heart of hearts" of those who seem to be favorable to the, 4) be self-conscious, 5) have no privacy, and 6) will defensively cower or display hostile bravado. In addition to claiming universality of its observations, Goffman's functionalist perspective decrees that its theories explain "hidden entities or properties" as well as past and "distant events." Thus, Goffman accounts for the "often secret" (p.9) quest of the stigmatized to attempt to correct the "failing." And Goffman concludes that his theory provides truth statements applicable at least in American society and at any time.

Ontological Concerns

Goffman assumes that the deaf and hearing exist in separate realities -- the former categorized as "discounted" and the latter categorized as "normal." He seeks to study both realties as distinct, focussing on the perception of deafness when both realities become "mixed contacts." He suggests that his theory predicts and controls these realities. This study rejects Goffman's functionalist ontological postulation, and the results suggest that the focus groups have multiple realities of (a) deaf culture, (b) racial cultures, (c) working class culture, and (d) high/low context culture. Thus, "prediction and control are unlikely outcomes although some level of understanding can be achieved" (Lincoln and Guba, 1985 p. 37).

Axiological and Epistemological Concerns

The functionalist approach to inquiry adopted by Goffman assumes that "inquiry is value-free and can be guaranteed to be so by virtue of the objective methodology employed" (Lincoln and Guba, 1985 p. 38). Also "classical science claims that theories and research are value-free; scholarship is neutral, attempting to get to the facts as they are manifest in the real world" (Littlejohn, 1992 p. 33). But, while this study recognizes the valuable contribution that Goffman has made in stigma research, the present researcher supports Littlejohn's (1992) assertion that, "when a scientist's values impinge on his or her work, the result is bad science." (p. 33) This study contends that "bad science" characterizes Goffman's work. Goffman imposes his values on his theory, and the following citations with emphasis added by this researcher are only a partial reflection of his value-laden treatise.

He refers to "... the stigmatized and **we normals** ..." (P.. 18), and quotes from a letter:

Dear Miss Lonely Hearts--
[I am] a ... girl ... born without a nose ... (introductory page unnumbered).
Referring to the girl, Goffman comments: "... **he** may continue through life to find that **he** ... . (p.19)

Goffman's value-laden theory has epistemological implications for "objectivity," an important criterion of functionalist inquiry which claims that "the inquirer and the object of inquiry are independent [as] the knower and the known constitute a discrete dualism" (Lincoln and Guba, 1985 p. 37).

Goffman's assertion of "we normals" who come into mixed contact with "shameful differentness" erases the independence of the knower and the known.

Goffman creates a separate reality for the deaf in a functionalist universe; assigns them the passive role of the "categorized," "tainted" and "discounted," assumes the role of both inquirer and the object of inquiry, represents his values in his theory creation, and uses his value-laden theory to control and predict the behavior of the deaf population. The variations in responses of the different groups of deaf individuals in the present study confirm that Goffman's theory is not generalizable.

Methodological Considerations

Goffman claims an isomorphistic relationship between deafness as causality and stigma as effect, not on the basis of conventional experimental design with rigidity of control, but on one shot case studies and autobiographies. Deterministic researchers Campbell and Stanley (1963) identify several weaknesses of the one shot case study contributing to findings which are "illusory upon analysis." They contend that it does not control for history, where attitudes may result from factors other than what the researcher is testing for; maturation, in which psychological processes vary over time; selection, accounting for extreme scores of subjects selected for their extremity; or mortality, in which there is a selective drop out of persons from the group. Thus they dismiss case studies as containing errors of "misplaced precision" and being of almost "no scientific value" (p. 6). They argue:

> How much more valuable the study would be if the one set of observations were reduced by half and the saved effort directed to the study in equal detail of an appropriate comparison instance. It seems well - nigh unethical at present to allow, as theses or dissertations [or theories] in education, case studies of this nature. (p. 6)

Kerlinger (1973) adds:

> It is doubtful that the investigators who use these designs are aware of their inadequacies ... [which] lead to no control or poor control of independent variables ... dangers cannot be avoided if they are not recognized ... scientifically speaking [the one shot case study] is worthless; worse, it can be badly misleading... . (pp. 317-318)

The present researcher questions the "validity" of Goffman's findings and the "reliability" of his generalizations that deafness is inevitably stigmatizing. He concludes a cause and effect relationship without accounting for sources of systematic variance. Second, this study posits that the extremely negative perception of physical and mental difference which Goffman identifies may have resulted from only selecting and representing individuals with extreme reactions to their conditions. Thus his high degree of correlation between the condition and stigma may be due not only to sources of variance but to errors of measurement. Third, Goffman's methodology does not account for maturation in which psychological processes vary over time. Glaser and Strauss (1967) question the operation of stigma over the course of individual lives, while Thompson (1982) seeks to understand what happens to stigma in intimate or long term encounters. Fourth, this study suggests that Goffman's theory does not account for cultural identification, which allows for individuals to "drop out" of the stigmatized group on the basis of a cultural bond and refute perceptions that their condition is negatively different. Campbell and Stanley (1963) identify history, maturation, and selection as among "main effects" factors in functionalist methodology which give the study internal validity and, where studies as those referenced by Goffman are internally invalid, the generalizability of findings are questionable.

Guided by the paradigmatic assumptions of naturalistic inquiry that: 1) realities are multiple, constructed, and holistic; 2) the inquirer and the "object" of inquiry interact to influence each other; 3) the aim of inquiry is to develop an idiographic body of knowledge in the form of working hypotheses that describe the individual case; and 4) all entities are in a state of mutual simultaneous shaping so that it is impossible to distinguish causes from effects (Lincoln and Guba, 1985 pp.37-38), this study not only criticizes Goffman's "theory of truth" that the deaf are inferior, anxious, and bewildered, but underscores the inappropriateness of the functionalist approach to understanding the flexibility of human behavior as it relates to persons who are deaf. The study suggests this on three levels: 1) Stigma is a transactional phenomenon; 2) stigma, deafness and culture are interrelated, and 3) selected deaf populations use constitutive and regulative rules in dealing with stigma.

STIGMA IS A TRANSACTIONAL PHENOMENON
(A) It is located in the sender

Goffman locates stigma in the recipient, but the present study locates it in the sender. The results show that three cultural groups, one of which is in a country other than the United States, all locate stigma in the sender or the "normal" and not in the individual with the condition perceived to be negatively different.   Members of the Jamaican deaf culture place responsibility for stigma not on their deafness, but on the hearing whom they claim give them "trouble." This very linguistic form, "giving trouble," shows that stigma does not always operate as Goffman claims.   The following excerpts from the Jamaican groups support this assertion as the Jamaicans identify trouble [stigma] as an externally imposed variable and not an internal response inherent in deafness.

Rose: "We don't know stigma but we know trouble. **That is what hearing people do to us**. They trouble us when they tease us ... when **they** laugh at us ... when **they** call us 'dummy' and **they** don't want to be with us or play with us. That is trouble" (emphasis added).

Jane: "We call it trouble. **They [persons who are hearing] trouble you [us]**" (emphasis added).

Steve: "I would like **hearing people to stop the trouble**. I would like **them** to stop calling me 'dummy.' I would like **them** to leave me alone, but **they** always give me trouble" (emphasis added).

Keba: "**Hearing people give deaf people a lot of trouble**. Sometimes I know when they are saying bad things about me because I watch their lips and, when they are done, I tell them to go away" (emphasis added).

John: "I sit down and watch hearing people talk, and **they call me a thief**, and I say, 'No. I am not a thief.' **They think because I am deaf, I do bad things, like stealing. They are liars and I don't think highly of them ...**" (emphasis added).

The African American group similarly locates stigma in the sender and not, as Goffman posits, in their deafness:

Carl: "It's funny when you sit back and watch hearing people. **They want to do the thinking for you, or assume that you don't know ...**" (emphasis added).

Dave: "When I was growing up, **hearing people would make fun of the way we signed. They mocked us ... made fun of us.** That happened many times, like I didn't fit into the scheme of things" (emphasis added).

Wayne: "Hearing people don't think we are equal ..."

Sandra: "... it is hard to communicate with hearing people because **they are always in a rush and it takes time for things to get interpreted ...**" (emphasis added).

With respect to White American deaf individuals as stigmatizers, the African Americans also locate stigma in the sender:

Carl: "... with White deaf people, **they** involve themselves with you for a short period of time ..." (emphasis added).

Kimal: "They [White deaf] trying to say you don't have enough deaf culture in you. I don't believe in that. I believe that if you have a hearing problem and you want to learn about deaf culture, you have a right" (emphasis added).

Sandra: "**White deaf people have a tendency to give us a lot of negative vibes** and we try to encourage people to have positive attitudes that Black deaf people can but White deaf people don't seem to think that way" (emphasis added).

The White American deaf also identify stigma as an external variable:

Helen: "**They** [hearing people] ask dumb questions like 'Do you drive?' **They** always confuse hearing [sic] with visual impairment. Or **they** discount us ..." (emphasis added).

Suzie: "They look down at you. **They** stare at you. You know, quite in your face. **They** invade our privacy or **they'll ask stupid questions** ..." (emphasis added).

Barbara: "I feel sorry for these people [hearing]. They are ignorant."

(B) Positive Perceptions of Deafness

Goffman claims that the stigmatized find that some of their own attributes warrant the denial of respect and regard enjoyed by "normals," and:

> in some cases it will be possible for him [sic] to make a direct attempt to correct what he sees as the objective basis of his failing ... where such repair is possible, what often results is not the acquisition of fully normal status, but a transformation of self from someone with a particular blemish into someone with a record of having corrected a particular blemish. (p. 9)

The present study confirms that there are deaf persons who neither regard deafness as "a failing" nor a condition which "needs repair." In fact, the three groups report feeling positive about their deafness.

Within the Jamaican groups:

Brad: "I feel good about myself. I feel some hearing people are stupid. ... sometimes we laugh at them when they think we are stupid because they are stupid to think we are stupid."

Sally: "It is okay to be deaf especially when we have deaf friends and family who love us. They understand me and I understand them." (Applause from every group member).

Grace: "Wait, let me talk about that! ... Hearing people are stupid. I laugh when they speak to me in mumble jumble because they think I am stupid that I don't understand. I laugh and they laugh because they think that I think that their mumble jumble is funny. But I laugh because they look stupid and behave stupid." (Applause from every member of the group).

John: "Nothing is wrong with deaf people. We have our friends and family and we feel good about ourselves."

Grace: "Some deaf people are famous ... like Miss America ... there are deaf dancers. Some deaf people win medals. Deaf people win speech competition in signing and travel around the world ..."

Within the African American group there are similar expressions:

Kimal: "I do not feel like deafness is a disability. I don't. I couldn't create myself. God did, and I am special. We are like everyone."

Wayne: "It is not a disability because we can do everything that hearing people can do. We just can't hear, that's all ..."

Bev: "Many deaf people can do anything. God made me special."

Within the White American group:

Vickie: "I'm really proud of being deaf. My family is deaf. We are very close to other deaf people ..."

Fay: "I look at hearing people and say they don't have anything. They don't know how we feel. So I feel proud of myself and all of us are from deaf families ..."

Burke: "I'm proud to be deaf ... yeah, yeah it's true. Maybe this will mess up your research study" (laughter).

Fay: "... sometimes I think deaf people know things in a different way, hearing people just hear sounds, but deaf people see things in a different way. That way we learn more."

(C) Deaf Persons are Agents in a Transaction

Goffman's theory which is attributional, negates interaction on the part of the stigmatized and denies them control over their responses to hearing persons. He claims that the "central feature of the stigmatized individual's life ... is 'acceptance' [by normals]"(p.8) [therefore] "... the stigmatized individual may find that he [sic] feels unsure of how we normals will identify him and receive him" (p.13).

Goffman argues that the stigmatized individual does not know (a) "which of several categories he [sic] will be placed in [by the 'normal']," (b) how the "normals" will be defining her "in their hearts" even where the placement is favorable, (c) if she is being scrutinized, "having to be self-conscious and calculating about the impression that he [sic] is making, to a degree and in areas of conduct which he [sic] assumes others are not" (p. 14), (d) when he [sic] will be approached at will by strangers who will nakedly expose him [sic] to invasions of privacy, and (e) if he [sic], in anticipation of negative attitudes towards him [sic], will anticipatorily respond by "defensive cowering" or "hostile bravado." On these bases, Goffman assigns a passive role to the stigmatized, describing them as "suspicious, depressed, hostile, anxious, and bewildered. Perry et al (1956) agree:

> The awareness of inferiority means that one is able to keep out of consciousness the formulation of some chronic feeling of the worst sort of insecurity, and this means that one suffers anxiety and perhaps even something worse, if jealousy is really worse than anxiety. The fear that others can disrespect a person because of something he [sic] shows means that he is always insecure in his contact with other people; and this insecurity arises, not from mysterious and somewhat disguised sources, as a great deal of our anxiety does, but from something he knows he cannot fix... . (p. 13)

This study disputes Goffman's claims and informs that members of the deaf culture do take control as agents in transactions between themselves and the hearing. The dominant view expressed in each group is not one of feeling inferior, depressed, hostile, anxious, nor bewildered as Goffman suggests. To the contrary, the study shows that some persons who are deaf are proud individuals who believe that hearing people who stigmatize them are stupid, uneducated, and need to be pitied. The following excerpts indicate that they also do not see communication as their problem but as the problem of the hearing.

Within the Jamaican group:

Keba: "... if they [the hearing] learnt Sign Language it would be better. All society should learn sign language" (applause).
John: "We try to use gestures and write notes to them but they still don't

understand. It is difficult to communicate with some hearing people."

Grace: "I communicate with some hearing ... mainly ... my teachers and my family.   It is difficult to use gestures because hearing people don't understand ... I still try."

Keba: "I want hearing people to learn Sign Language and I will teach anyone who wants to learn. They must learn to respect deaf people ..."

Craig: "... my parents don't deal with deafness. They don't sign. They can't communicate with me and I get angry."

Brad: "Hearing people should try and communicate with deaf people. They should learn to sign."

Jim: "All policemen and doctors. Everybody should learn sign. When I write, they don't understand and it is difficult for me ..."

Joy: "Hearing people are good, but they need to learn sign language so that they can communicate with us and understand us. Doctors, policemen especially" (applause from each group member).

Within the African American Group:

Wayne: "Now sometimes I think hearing people do not have a lot of patience because they cannot understand deaf communication ..."

Sandra: "For example in the library, someone came up and asked me a question and, when he found out I was deaf, he just turned away and left. It didn't bother me."

Kimal: "... Giving [getting] too much expression [from hearing persons] bothers me, and then I get an attitude. But if it looks like they really want to do something, then I can reciprocate."

Carl: "Hearing people should learn about deaf culture. There are books at the book store, they can read. For example, you have come here to learn about deaf culture. You are motivated. I would like to see other hearing people do the same."

Kimal: "They should learn to respect us" (applause).

Within the White American group, the consensus was that they do not think it necessary to facilitate communication with the hearing:

Burke: "We are different. We have our own values. We carry on a tradition."

Fay: "We can never become oralists in a hearing world. We are different and proud of who we are."

Barbara: "... hearing people (mimics a patronizing tone) 'want to learn sign language so they can help us' (laughter)!"

Fay: "They keep coming up and asking us: 'How do you sign this? How do you sign that?' Well excuse me, but I just don't have the time to do that! I'm sorry! If they want to learn about the deaf, get involved with the culture!"

Second, deaf persons take control, deliberately rejecting and selecting persons with whom they wish to communicate.

Jamaicans:

Keba: "Sometimes we meet hearing people who sign and we communicate with them. But it's hard to manage [when the hearing do not sign] because hearing people have no understanding of us".

John: "I communicate only with my hearing family, my teachers and some people at the Seventh Day Adventist Church ..."

June: "I don't communicate a lot with hearing people. Only those that I must. Like my grandmother."

Edna: "I communicate with people who are deaf. Not much hearing. Only my mother and father."

African Americans:

Wayne: "... sometimes they [hearing people] think it [communicating with the deaf] is taking too much time. If they don't have the patience then they leave. I don 't stop them."

Dave: "... I don't waste time with them ..."

Kimal: "If they want to give up and have a bad attitude, I just leave it. That's their way."

Carl: "Sometimes they offend me, but once they play dumb with me, I play dumb with them too."

Within the White American group:

Every member agrees with Fay's summary of the control they exert in their communication interaction with the hearing.

Fay: "We can never become oralists in a hearing world. We are different and proud of who we are. [Therefore] when they keep coming up and asking us 'How do you sign this? How do you sign that?' Well excuse me, but I just don't have the time to do that! I'm sorry! If they want to learn about the deaf, get involved with the culture!"

Third, this study confirms that some persons who are deaf neither "defensively cower" nor display "hostile bravado" as Goffman advises but on the contrary demand respect from the hearing or ignore them completely.

Jamaicans:

Jane: "... I fight back. I quarrel with them. The hearing should not do this to us. But then after I fight a little, I just stop and ignore them."

Rose: "I feel like fighting them sometimes ..."

Sally: "When I was ten years old, I couldn't ride my bicycle so my hearing friends laughed and said, 'You can't ride bicycle.' One day I tried and tried. I fall off, but I tried again. When I could ride, I told my friends that I could ride and they said, 'Let's see.' And when they saw me riding, everyone was surprised."

Jim: "We ignore hearing people when they trouble us. We ignore them a lot."

Sally: "Sometimes we ignore them because they always start the trouble..."

Greta: "... we laugh at hearing people ... sometimes."

John: "... we laugh and call them fools in Sign Language."

Max: "I think hearing people are stupid because when they don't want to play football with me, what does that have to do with anything? What does deafness have to do with kicking a ball? They are so stupid!"

John: "... deaf people are better off with each other."

Keba: "... they must learn to respect Deaf people."

Sarah: "One hearing man in a shop started speaking dirty to me and make sexual gestures. I signed to him that, if he continued, I was going to punch him. I quarreled with him and I quarrel with them all the time when they pinch me on my bottom and when they speak dirty to me. I fight. They must not do that. They must respect me. They take advantage of me because I am deaf, but I will not let them do that. I fight back."

Max: "When they give me trouble, I curse them."

Greta: "Well, I fight them, because if they fight me, what am I supposed to do?"

Joy: "I am innocent. They are guilty, so I ignore them."

African Americans:

Carl: "... it's funny when you sit back and watch hearing people. They want to do the thinking for you..."

Sandra: "... when I asked them [to explain] they would go 'Oh God, I will tell you later.' ... I didn't want to interact with that kind of hearing person ... it takes time for things to get interpreted ..."

Kimal: "... if they want to ... have a bad attitude, I just leave it."

Carl: "Hearing people should learn about deaf culture."

Kimal: "They should learn to respect us" (applause).

Wayne: "Hearing people don't think we are equal so we fight."

Question: "How do you fight?"

Sandra: "By approaching people directly and telling them what we want." (They all nod in agreement.)

Wayne: "Like my sister ... she yelled at me, 'I wish my brother wasn't deaf. He's so stupid.' And I said, 'Go ahead, insult me, it doesn't bother me. I'm your brother. You're my sister and you have to accept the way your brother is. Period. That's all you've got. That's all I've got.' "

White Americans:

Barbara: "... some hearing people are stupid ..."

Helen: "We just like... to the question, do you drive? We say, 'Yes of course. We can see the road ...' "

Vickie: "I'm really proud of being deaf ..."

Burke: "... I'm proud to be deaf ..."

Barbara: "[Some] hearing people (she mimics a patronizing tone) want to learn Sign Language so they can help us (laughter)."

Fay: "... well excuse me ... if they want to learn about the deaf, get involved with the culture" (every member agrees).

Burke: "We are different. We have our own values. We carry on a tradition."

Fay: "We are different and proud of who we are [and] ... I look at hearing people and say ... they don't know how we feel ... we have much better self esteem ..."

The researcher suggests and the data confirm that stigma is transactional. Some deaf individuals report that communication is not their problem, but the problem of the hearing; that they have positive perceptions of themselves as deaf individuals; and that they are not passive but actively engage as agents in the transaction between themselves and the hearing.

The Fifth Communication Concern

The present researcher concludes that Goffman's analysis dismisses the role culture plays in the perception of negative difference. He argues:

> Knowing from their own experience what it is like to have this particular stigma, some of them can provide the individual with instruction in the tricks of the trade, and with a circle of lament to which he [sic] can withdraw for moral support and for the comfort of feeling at home, at ease, accepted as a person who really is like any other normal person. (p.20)

Goffman describes these groups as categories but acknowledges conceptual confusion in the application of the term. Culture should never be considered a "category" especially when such categorization is critical in arriving at epistemological assumptions. Culture is not merely a unit but is the basis of reality as "... within a social group or culture, reality is defined not so much by individual acts, but by complex and organized patterns of ongoing actions" (Gergen, 1985 pp. 266-269). Goffman argues that often, in such categories, individuals will neither have a capacity for collective action nor a stable and embracing pattern of mutual interaction. The data in this study suggest differently, as where individuals consider themselves part of a culture, not only are they not in a circle of lament, but they have common behaviors and attitudes which reject stigmatizing behaviors. However, this researcher recognizes that Goffman's analysis may be applicable to individuals who do not consider themselves part of a culture but reminds that the focus of this study remains on the impact of culture on stigma and the relationship between culture, stigma, and deafness.

Culture, Stigma, and Deafness Interrelated

The data confirm that differences in culture do affect how individuals who are deaf deal with the perception that deafness is negatively different. Research evidence in the present study indicates that the Jamaicans interviewed identify themselves as part of a deaf culture and, in so far as their positive beliefs about themselves are reinforced and supported by friends and family, they do not feel stigmatized. Indeed, deaf culture members boast about being third generation deaf and hope for deaf children. When persons are not regarded as important to the communication process, then they are ignored by the Jamaican deaf culture.

The researcher also notes that the parents, teachers and other authority figures within the Jamaican working class culture influence the communication choices that the deaf culture makes, advising its members to ignore stigmatizing behaviors. In addition, the Jamaicans report that within the high context culture of their environment they focus on the context of the interaction to define meanings. The investigation also revealed that these Jamaicans regard stigmatizers as stupid and suggest that many communication problems could be avoided if hearing persons learned sign language.

The study found that the African American deaf interviewed are ambivalent about their roles as members of the deaf culture. This ambivalence accounts for different behaviors towards stigma from the hearing community generally and the White American deaf specifically. While they make communication choices which include ignoring hearing persons who stigmatize them, the data suggest that the group interviewed has not yet developed combative strategies to deal with stigmatizing behaviors of the White American deaf. Thus as a group, they continue to feel stigmatized by their white peers.

The data describe the White Americans who are deaf as having a high self esteem. Of the three groups represented, they report themselves to be the least stigmatized. Consciousness of themselves as a deaf culture determines their relationship with others and their attitudes towards stigma. This group is the least accommodating of hearing persons generally and stigmatizers specifically, and the data describe them as recognizing their cultural differences and traditions. Both American groups report that within the low context culture of American society they derive meaning from the content of messages. Not only are stigma, culture and deafness linked but, where there is a greater level of cultural consciousness of deafness, the more likely it is that such culturally aware deaf individuals will reject stigma. Investigating the study's fifth communication concern, the researcher finds that cultural variability exists in the perception of negative difference and that Goffman's thesis does not account for this. This finding contradicts Goffman's claim: "A good portion of those who fall within a given stigma category ... will neither have a capacity for collective action, nor a stable and embracing pattern of mutual interaction. ..." (p.23) Cultural variability not only removes the deaf from passivity but introduces the role of culture into the analysis of stigma.

Constitutive and Regulative Rules
Dealing with Stigma

The study confirms that the selected deaf populations use constitutive and regulative rules in dealing with stigmatization. With reference to the African Americans, the researcher identified rule guided behaviors common to their deaf culture. These are 1) making an effort to communicate only with those hearing individuals who express a genuine need and desire to communicate with the deaf and 2) ignoring others. With respect to their personal communication world view choices, the study found that these choices include 1) "fighting for equality" with hearing persons and 2) making personal adjustment to "racist attitudes." One individual reported "fighting [engaging in physical confrontation]." Within an interethnic context, the rule of their culture was to avoid stigmatizing behaviors of the White deaf and "go on with our lives."

The Jamaican groups recognized that stigmatizing behaviors come primarily from adults. They identified two rule - guided behaviors that they use in responding to stigma: 1) to communicate only with those "hearing persons necessary" and 2) to ignore others (who do not play an important role in their lives). In both Jamaican groups, communication world view choices of individuals include "reasoning [with the stigmatizer]" and "avoiding"[them]. Each group had one individual who indicated "fighting [physically confronting the stigmatizer]." Within the working class culture, the researcher identified a cultural rule as both Jamaican groups report that parents, teachers, and some hearing persons urge them to ignore stigmatizing behaviors and thus avoid conflict.

The White American group indicated that stigmatizing behaviors come from the hearing culture generally but more so from the hearing whites in Junior High School. The study also identified cultural rules which determined behavior common to the White American group.

1) The deaf can never be oralists in a hearing world.
2) Communication with the deaf is the responsibility of the hearing.
3) If the hearing culture wishes to communicate with the deaf culture, it should make the effort to learn about the deaf culture.
4) Pity those who regard the deaf as negatively different.

These rules also account for similar personal communication world view choices. However, one individual who reported adhering to the cultural rules of behavior also felt the urge to express herself in another way: "I feel angry ... sometimes I wish I could ..." She refused to say what she wished she could do, but the researcher speculates that she perhaps wished she could physically confront stigmatizers as was done by one individual in each group interviewed. In an interethnic context, the researcher also identified a cultural rule which guides their behavior: "... They [Blacks] think of themselves as Black first, and deaf after ... we feel deaf first and then White ... that's the difference... ."

The theory of the Coordinated Management of Meaning not only provided a framework to identify the rules and behaviors, but it allowed the data to indicate the extent to which the groups of deaf individuals are in coordination with the rest of society. The essence of coordination, as discussed in Chapter 2, is that "people can have perfectly satisfactory coordination without understanding one another ... [in the interaction] both sides are satisfied and each thinks what happened is appropriate... ." (Littlejohn, 1992 p. 207). Coordination for the deaf and hearing cultures therefore arises when they are able to interact within the same context but without the need to understand or agree with each other's perception of deafness.

Interethnic Aspects of Deafness

The study confirms that deafness has a racial aspect as the African American deaf feel that the White deaf exclude them from the deaf culture.

Sandra: "Within our [deaf culture] we are discriminated against..."

Kimal: "Growing up as a deaf person, I never faced much problem. It wasn't until I came to Gallaudet that I saw the separation. I was really surprised about this deaf culture thing and the differences ... White deaf people have a tendency to give us a lot of negative vibes ... like they feel like Black deaf people can't participate in the student body government and in other organizations. They kinda give a lot of excuses as to why you can't get in the program..."

Carl: "You feel like you are not welcome. You feel like you're not getting the kinds of services that you need..."

Kimal: "It's like white deaf people here at Gallaudet can accept gays and lesbians, but they can't accept you being Black and deaf. I don't get it."

The African Americans who are deaf conceptualize their relationship with the White deaf as being in a hostile environment over which they have no control, and therefore they focus on survival.

Sandra: "I'm from New York City, and I went to a deaf school. The first time I came to Gallaudet I had a white room mate ... During the first semester, she wanted me to move so she could have a new [white] room mate. She said she couldn't move because she had back problems, and I said, 'well, I've got back problems, too.' To survive the situation, I went ahead and moved out ..."

Dave: "I don't feel like I'm getting any positive support from whites here. It's always very negative ..."

Wayne: "We just deal with this racism ... we are used to it ... we don't let it interrupt our lives. We just kinda go on with our lives."

The African Americans who are deaf take much less agency and control in dealing with racial stigma than they do with deaf stigma. This may be due to the fact that as racial stigma was once legislated, it is more embedded in the fabric of American society. Thus, it is more offensive to, and controlling of, African American deaf persons than the stigma of deafness. Further, in the present era of political correctness, African American deaf individuals may find it more difficult to confront racist behaviors which are now more subtle. In addition, African American deaf who compare themselves with African American hearing persons may find that the latter still do not have much agency and control over racial stigma. Also, African Americans, both deaf and hearing, belong to a racial minority with comparatively far less economic and political influence in the United States.   On the contrary, White Americans who are deaf belong to the majority culture which share economic and political power in the United States. Thus, this study suggests that African Americans may exert more agency in dealing with deaf stigma because they perceive that they have more control and a greater level of success in managing issues relating to deafness.

Whereas the African Americans who are deaf see racial stigma as controlled by the white American deaf, the White Americans who are deaf view the racial stigma of deafness as external to them. This perspective is similar to the one they have of deaf stigma which they identify as being the problem of the hearing society:

Fay: "When Black deaf people say they are not deaf enough to be part of the culture, I think that's just a racist attitude. They look at everything in terms of race..."

Burke: "It doesn't have anything to do with deafness because we [Black and White] are both deaf. It has to do with race and attitude."

Barbara: "The SBG is open to volunteers, but who comes to volunteer? Most of the time they, the Blacks, don't volunteer. So in a way they're kinda asking for it."

Burke: "Sometimes we have interviews for positions on the SBG. The competition is high, so I can only pick one person, and I pick the best person and most of the time he happens to be white ..."

Since the White American deaf do not claim control of racism in the relationship between themselves and the African American deaf, they do not feel themselves responsible to be the agents of change. The study posits further that the relationship between both groups of deaf individuals at Gallaudet reflects a balance of forces similar to that which exists between African American and White American groups at the macro level. The White Americans who are deaf might, therefore, feel that their responses to the African Americans who are deaf do not violate interracial relationships.

Cultural identity is based on deafness for Whites, nationality for Jamaicans, and race for African Americans. This raises the issue of identity negotiation among groups of deaf individuals. Where groups of deaf individuals belong to a macro culture which becomes a "parent culture," they negotiate their identity mainly on the level of cultural difference from the macro culture. For example, in the case of the White American deaf, the "parent culture" is White American but because this culture is standardized and accepted, a white deaf individual negotiates her identity on deafness. If there are other levels of difference from the standardized culture, such an individual would negotiate those levels appropriately. Thus a White individual might not only be deaf, but woman and lesbian, and would have to deal with each level of cultural difference.

In the case of Jamaicans, the macro or parent culture is standardized as nationality, and therefore the Jamaicans negotiate their identity on deafness -- the cultural difference from the parent culture. Hence, the Jamaicans report themselves as deaf. African Americans, perceive themselves as Black first.

Race is the cultural difference that requires the greatest identity negotiation for this group. However, their macro or parent culture, as well as cultural code-switching by deaf groups, need to be examined in future research.

Strengths of the Study

The study disputes Goffman's functionalist approach on the following bases: 1) an ontology of separateness does not exist between deaf and hearing persons; 2) his theory can not always predict and control the realties of deaf individuals; 3) a discrete dualism does not exist between himself as an inquirer and the mixed contact of deaf and hearing persons as the observed; and 4) deafness does not always cause stigma. The present study also notes that Goffman's methodology is based on case studies which functionalist researchers dismiss as "scientifically worthless."

The study also reveals that stigma is transactional. Persons who are deaf locate stigma in the sender and, as they exert control over their communication interactions, they become agents in the transaction between themselves and hearing persons, demanding respect, and establishing communication limits. Second, persons who are deaf and regard themselves as part of the deaf culture are proud of their cultural identity and do not defensively cower as Goffman suggests. Third, the metatheoretical assumptions of the interpretive paradigm guided the study to facilitate the emergence of another perspective on stigma from the voices of persons who are deaf and not from a nomothetic covering law. Thus, the data reveal how these individuals feel about themselves, how they feel about deafness, how they feel about hearing individuals, how they feel about culture, and how they feel about stigma. Fourth, cultural variability exists in the perception that deafness is negatively different and that Goffman's analysis does not account for this. This finding contradicts Goffman's claim that "a good portion of those who fall within a given stigma category ... will neither have the capacity for collective action, nor a stable and embracing pattern of mutual interaction ..." (p.23). Fifth, culturally different deaf groups use regulative and constitutive rules in dealing with stigma and are at different levels of co-ordination with the hearing society. Sixth, in the interethnic context, deafness has a racial aspect. In this regard, Whites regard themselves as deaf first and African Americans regard themselves as Black first. Thus, cultural identity is based on deafness for Whites, and race for African Americans.

The study also shows that deaf cultures engage in identity negotiation and suggests that they negotiate their identity mainly on the levels of what makes them culturally different from the macro culture. The study also identified different cultural behaviors relative to the high and low context nature of societies as well as to class position in society. In the high context culture of Jamaica, deaf persons focus on the context of the interaction to derive meaning, while in the low context culture of the United States, meaning is derived from the content of messages. Within the working class culture, the Jamaicans who are deaf report that respect for authority figures influence their attitudes towards the hearing.

Limitations

The researcher notes three limitations to the study. First, with only an introductory knowledge of American and Jamaican Sign Languages, she had to rely on the representations of interpreters. She had little way of verifying the accuracy of the material interpreted, though she could follow the topics. Second, as a hearing individual, the researcher was aware that cultural differences between the hearing and the deaf might have reduced the confidence level of the interactants in the researcher's ability to "represent their views." Third, as a Jamaican of African descent, the researcher was also aware of ethnic differences between herself and the white American group which might have raised the latter's suspicion as to her motives and intentions for doing the study.

Recommendations

(1) For Jamaicans

As part of its proposed constitutional legislation on matters concerning individuals who are disabled, the Jamaican Government could (a) require all schools to introduce the instruction of the Jamaican Sign Language as part of their curriculum; (b) require that professional bodies such as the Jamaica Constabulary Force and the Nurses Association of Jamaica introduce the instruction of Jamaican Sign Language in their training programs; and (c) make additional grants available for research on deafness in Jamaica.

(2) For African and White American Groups

African American and White American researchers who are deaf could conduct collaborative research in the cultural relationships between both groups with a view to recommending ways in which the relationship between the groups may be improved. The research teams should include both White and Black researchers.

(3) For Howard University

This researcher suggests that, as a pioneer college providing instruction primarily for hearing students of African descent as well as for deaf students including African Americans, Howard University provide assistive learning devices for hard of hearing students as well as interpreting services in the classrooms for those students who are profoundly deaf. Howard University should also establish a deaf program providing courses on the deaf culture as well as provide increased instruction in Sign Language. The present Sign Language course which is sometimes offered in the summer semester is not adequate but should be part of a total educational package on deaf education.

Future Research

The results of this study raise two particularly important issues for future research. First, how do other racial groups of deaf individuals compare with African Americans and White Americans? What are their strategies for dealing with stigma? Second, to what extent and with what implications do identity negotiation and cultural code switching occur among culturally deaf groups?

Research into these issues would provide further insight into the multiple realities of deaf groups and how they deal with stigma. Lincoln and Guba's (1985) guidelines would be particularly helpful for doing this research. They propose that interested researchers be guided by the naturalist paradigm in their investigation, as this will not only provide for the richness of a discourse within the contexts of the perspective of the groups but will also enable the investigator to deal with the multiple realities which exist. Further, the researcher should interact with the group members who will become respondents. This will enable a better understanding of the issues being addressed. The setting will also enable the investigator to identify subtle behaviors and nuances important to the issues being debated. The investigator should consider purposive sampling as well as inductive data analysis. A grounded theory should be allowed to develop from the data as this will best account for the realities of the respondents. The research design should emerge "because it is inconceivable that enough could be known ahead of time about the many multiple realities to devise the design adequately ..." (p. 41). The investigator should recognize that her function is to reconstruct "their constructions of reality" as "inquiry outcomes depend upon the nature and quality of the interaction between the knower and the known, epitomized in negotiations about the meaning of data..." . (p.41)

Conclusion

This study, by taking an interpretive approach to a problem traditionally examined through a functionalist lens, has revealed the agency and strength of self which exists in individuals in deaf communities. Far from the cowering, self-hating flotsam of Goffman's analysis, these individuals who are deaf exert tremendous control in their social world. Stigma is not a necessary attachment to a negatively valued difference but rather a social phenomenon which emerges when social transactions occur between individuals who inhabit different worlds.

Appendix

DISABILITY

Definition

In the context of health experience, disability is any restriction or lack (resulting from an impairment) of ability to perform an activity in the manner or within the range considered normal for a human being.

Characteristics

Disability is characterized by excesses or deficiencies of customarily expected activity performance and behavior, and these may be temporary or permanent, reversible or irreversible, and progressive or regressive. Disabilities may arise as a direct consequence of impairment or as a response by the individual, particularly psychologically, to a physical, sensory, or other impairment. Disability represents objectification of impairment and as such it reflects disturbances at the level of the person.

Disability is concerned with abilities, in the form of composite activities and behaviors, that are generally accepted as essential components of everyday life. Examples include disturbances in behaving in an appropriate manner, in personal care (such as excretory control and the ability to wash and feed one's self), in the performance of other activities of daily living, and in locomotor activities such as the ability to walk.

Communication Disabilities

This refers to an individual's ability to generate and emit messages and to receive and understand messages.

SPEAKING DISABILITIES
Disability in understanding speech
Includes: loss or restriction of the ability to understand the meaning of verbal messages.
Excludes: listening disabilities and situation-related difficulties such as lack of knowledge of a local language.
Disability in talking
Includes: loss or restriction of the ability to produce audible verbal messages and to convey meaning through speech.
Other speaking disability
Disability in understanding other audible messages
Excludes: listening disabilities
Disability in expression through substitute language codes
Includes: loss or restriction of the ability to convey information by a code of sign language.
Other disability with substitute language codes
Includes: loss or reduction of the ability to receive information by a code of sign language.

LISTENING DISABILITIES
Disability in listening to speech
Includes: loss or reduction of the ability to receive verbal messages.
Other listening disability
Includes: loss or reduction of the ability to receive other audible messages.

SEEING DISABILITIES
Disability in gross visual tasks
Includes: loss or reduction of the ability to execute tasks requiring adequate distant or peripheral vision.
Disability in detailed visual tasks
Includes: loss or reduction of the ability to execute tasks requiring adequate visual acuity, such as reading, recognition of faces,

writing, and visual manipulation.

Other disability in seeing and related activities

Disability in night vision

Disability in colour recognition

Disability in comprehending written messages

Includes: loss or reduction of the ability to decode and understand written messages.

Other disability in reading written language

Includes: difficulty with speed or endurance

Disability in reading other systems of notation

Includes: loss or reduction of the ability to read Braille by an individual disabled in near sight, who had previously had this ability, or difficulty in learning this system of notation by an individual disabled in near sight.

Disability in lip reading

Includes: loss or reduction of the ability to lip-read by an individual disabled in listening who had previously had this ability, or difficulty in learning this skill by an individual disabled in listening.

Disability in writing

Includes: loss or reduction of the ability to encode language into written words and to execute written messages or to make marks.

References

Ablon, J. (1990). Ambiguity and difference: Families with dwarf children. *Social Science and Medicine, 30*, 8, 879-887.

Ainlay, S.C., Becker, G., & Coleman, L.M. (1986). *The dilemma of difference: A multidisciplinary view of stigma.* Plenum Press. New York & London.

Alder, A. (1990). *Problems of neurosis.* New York: Cosmopolitan Book Co.

Allport, G.W. (1958). *The nature of prejudice.* New York: Doubleday Anchor Books. Doubleday and Company Inc.

Anspach, R. R. (1979). From stigma to identity politics: Political activism among the physically disabled and former mental patients. *Social Science and Medicine, 13A*, 765-772.

Applegate, J. L., and Sypher, H. E. (1983). A constructivist outline. In *Intercultural communication theory: Current perspectives.* William B. Gudykunst. (Ed.). Beverly Hills, Calif.: Sage.

Applegate, J. L., and Sypher, H. E. (1988). A constructionist theory of communication and culture. In *Theories in intercultural communication*, Young Kim and William Gudykunst (Eds.). Newbury Park, Calif.: Sage.

Asch, A. (1984). The experience of disability: A challenge for psychology. *American Psychologist. 39*, 529-536.

Ashmore, R.D. and Del Boca, F.K. (1976). Psychological approaches to understanding intergroup conflicts. In P.A. Katz (Ed.). *Towards the elimination of racism*, 73-123. New York: Pergamon.

Bandura, A. (1977). *Social learning theory*. Englewood Cliffs, NJ.: Prentice-Hall.

Barker, R.G. (1948). The Social psychology of physical disability. In L. Meyerson (Ed.), *Journal of Social Issues. 4*, 4, 28-38.

Barker, R.G., Wright, B.A.; Meyerson, L., & Gonnick M.R. (1953). *Adjustment to physical handicap and illness: A survey of the social psychology of physique and disability.* (2nd Edition) New York. Social Science Research Council.

Berger, C.R. and Calabrese, R.J. (1975). Some explorations in initial interactions and beyond. *Human Communication Research, 1,* 99-112.

Bernstein, B. (1971). *Class, codes, and control: Theoretical studies toward a sociology of language.* London.

Best, J., and Luckenbill, D.F. (1980). The social organization of deviants. *Social Problems, 28,* 1, (October), 14-31.

Brickman, P., Rabonovitz, V.C., Karuza, J., Coates, D., Cohn, E., and Kiddler, L. (1982). Models of helping and coping. *American Psychologist, 37,* 368-384.

Bulman, R., Wortman, C. (1977). Attributions of blame and coping in the real world: Severe accident victims react to their lot. *Journal of Personality and Social Psychology, 35,* 351-363.

Bynder, H., New, K-M. (1976). Time for a change: From micro to macro sociological concepts in disability research. *Journal of Health and Social Behavior, 17,* 1, 45-52 (March).

Cain, L.F. (1948). The disabled child in school. In L. Meyerson (Ed.), *Journal of Social Issues*, 4, 4. 90-93.

117

Campbell, D.T., Stanley, J.C. (1963). *Experimental and quasi-experimental designs for research.* Rand McNally College Publishing Co.: Chicago.

Cook, T.D., Campbell, D.T. (1979). *Quasi experimentation: Design and analysis issues for field settings.* Chicago: Rand McNally.

Cronbach, L.J. (1975). *Beyond the two disciplines of scientific psychology.* American Psychologist, 30, 116-127.

Cronen, V.E., and Shuter, R. (1983). Forming intercultural bonds. In *Intercultural Communication Theory: Current Perspectives.* Gudykunst, W. (Ed.). Newbury Park, Calif. Sage, 1988.

Cruickshank, William M. (1948). The impact of physical disability on social adjustment. In L. Meyerson (Ed.), *Journal of Social Issues, 4,* 4, 78-83.

Cutsforth, D.T. (1948). Personality crippling through physical disability. In L. Meyerson (Ed.), *Journal of Social Issues, 4,* 4. 62-67.

Davis, B. (1989). Attitudes towards disabled children in St. Kitts. *Conquest, 2,* 3-4.

Davis, F. (1961). Deviance disavowal: The management of strained interaction by the visibly handicapped. *Social Problems, 9,* 2. 120-133.

Davis, F. (1972). Deviance Disavowal: The management of strained interaction by the visibly handicapped. In *Illness, interaction, and the Self.* Davis, F. (Ed.), 133-149. Wadsworth. Belmont.

Davis, N. (1975). *Sociological construction of deviance: Perspectives and issues in the field.* Brown, New York.

Dembo, T., Leviton, G.L., and Wright, B.A. (1975). Adjustment to misfortune: A problem of social psychological rehabilitation. *Rehabilitation Psychology. 22,* 1. Reprinted *Final Report to the Army Medical Research and Development Board.* Office of the Surgeon General, War Department, April 1948.

Deutsch, M. (1985). *Distributive justice.* New Haven, CT. Yale University Press.

DeWeaver, K.L. (1983). Deinstitutionalization of the developmentally disabled. *Social Work.* (November-December), 435-439.

Dodd, C. H. (1991). *Dynamics of intercultural communication.* Third Edition. Wm. C. Brown Publishers.

Dubrow, A. L. (1965). Attitudes towards people with disability. *Journal of Rehabilitation. 31,* 4, 25-26.

Dworkin, A., & Dworkin, R. (Eds.) (1976). *The minority report.* New York: Praeger.

Edgerton, R.B. (1970). Mental retardation in non-western societies: Toward a cross-cultural perspective on incompetence. In H.C. Haywood (Ed.), *Socio-cultural aspects of mental retardation.* New York: Appleton-Century-Crofts.

Embree, J. (1946). *A Japanese village.* Chicago: University of Chicago Press.

Erting, C. J., Johnson, R.C., Smith, D.L., Snider, R.E. (1994). *The deaf way.* Gallaudet University Press.

Exline, R. V. and Winters, L.C. (1965). Affective relations and mutual glances in dyads. In S.S. Thomkins and C.E. Izard (Eds.). *Affect, cognition, and personality.* New York. Springer.

Fletcher, C.M.A. (1992). Changing attitudes. *Conquest,* 4, 2&3, 3-4.

Force, D.G. (1956). Social status of physically handicapped children. *Exceptional children, 23,* 104-108

Ford, J. (1975). *Paradigms and fairy tales.* Routeledge and Kegan Paul.

Fine, M., and Asch, A. (1988). Disability beyond stigma: Social interaction, discrimination and activism. *Journal of Social Issues, 44,* 1, 3-21.

Fletcher, C. (1992). Changing Attitudes. *Conquest, 14,* (2 & 3), 16-20.

Frank, G. (1988). Beyond Stigma: Visibility and self-empowerment of persons with congenital limb deficiencies. *Journal of Social Issues, 44,* 1. 1988, 95-115.

Gaier, E. L., Linkowski, D.C., and Jacques, M. E. (1967). Contact as a variable in the perception of disability. *Journal of Social Psychology, 74,* 117-126.

Gannon, J. R. (1989). *The week the world heard Gallaudet.* Gallaudet University Press. Washington, D.C.

Gennep A. Van. (1960). *The rites of passage.* University of Chicago Press. Chicago. Il.

Gergen, K.J.(1985). The social constructionist movement in modern psychology. *American Psychologist, 40,* 266-275.

Glaser, B.G., and Strauss, A.L. (1967). *The discovery of grounded theory: Strategies for qualitative research.* Chicago. Aldine.

Gluckman, M. (1962). *Essays on the ritual of social relations.* Manchester, England: Manchester University Press.

Goffman, E. (1963). *Stigma: Notes on the management of spoiled identity.* Englewood Cliffs, New Jersey: Prentice Hall.

Granofsky, J. (1955). *Modification of attitudes towards the visibly disabled: An experimental study of the effectiveness of social contact in producing a modification of the attitudes of nondisabled females toward visibly disabled males.* Unpublished dissertation. Yeshiva University, New York: New York.

Groce, N. (1985). *Everyone here spoke sign language: Hereditary deafness on Martha's vineyard.* Cambridge, MA.: Harvard University Press.

Gudykunst, W.B. (1988). Uncertainty and anxiety. In *Theories of intercultural communication.* Kim, Y.Y. and Gudykunst, W.B. (Eds.). Newbury Park, Calif.: Sage.

Gudykunst, W.B. and Young Y.K. (1984). *Communicating with strangers.* New York: Random House.

Gussow, Z. and Tracey, G. (1968). Status, ideology, and adaptation to stigmatized illness: A study of leprosy. *Human Organization, 27.* 4, 316-325.

Hahn, H. (1985). Towards a politics of disability: Definitions, disciplines, and policies. *The Social Science Journal, 22,* 4, 87-105, (October).

Hairston, E. and Smith, L. (1983). *Black and deaf in America: Are we that different?* T.J. Publishers. Maryland.

Hall, E.T. (1959). *The silent language.* Garden City, NY: Doubleday.

Hall, E.T., (1966). *The hidden dimension.* New York: Random House.

Hanks, J. R., & Hanks, L.M. (1948). The physically handicapped in certain non-occidental societies. *Journal of Social Issues, 4.* 4, 11-19.

Hardaway, B. (1988). *Silent Avoidance: The relationship between attitudes and physical impairments among deaf students.* Doctoral dissertation. Howard University.

Hardaway, B. (1990). Imposed inequality and miscommunication between physically impaired and physically nonimpaired interactants in American Society. *The Howard Journal of Communications, 3,* 139-148. (Summer/Fall 1991).

Hecht, M. L., Anderson, P. A., and Ribeau, S. A. (1989). *The cultural dimensions of nonverbal communication.* In Handbook of International and Intercultural Communication. Asante, M. K. and Gudykunst, W. B. (Eds.). Newbury Park, Calif. Sage.

Hess, M. (1980). *Revolutions and reconstructions in the philosophy of science.* Bloomington: Indiana University Press.

Higgins, P. C. (1980). *Outsiders in a hearing world.* Sage. California. London.

Hofstede, G. (1984). *Culture's consequence: International differences in work-related values*. Beverly Hills, CA: Sage.

Holy Bible, King James Version (1979). Leviticus, Chapter 21; verses 16-23. Holman Bible Publishers, Nashsville, TN.

Homans, G.L. (1950). *The Human Group*. New York: Harcourt, Brace and World.

Horowitz, I. and Liebowitz, M. (1968). Social Deviance and Political Marginality. *Social Problems*, 281-296.

Infante, D.A.; Rancer S.A; Womack, D.F. (1990). *Building Communication Theory*. Waveland Press. Inc. Illinois.

Jacques, M. E., Linkowski, D.C. and Sieka, F.L. (1970). Cultural attitudes toward disability - Denmark, Greece and United States. *International Journal of Social Psychiatry, 16,* 54-62.

Jankowski, K. (1991). On communicating with deaf people. In *Intercultural Communication*. A Reader. Samovar, L. and Porter, R. (Eds.).

Jenness, D. (1959). *The people of the twilight*. Chicago: University of Chicago Press.

Jensen, E. (1974). *The Iban and their religion*. Oxford, England: Oxford University Press.

Jones, E.E., Farina, A., Hastorf, A.H., Markus, H., Miller, D.T., Scott, R.A., and French, R. de S., (1984). *Social Stigma: The psychology of marked relationships*. New York. Freeman.

Journal of Social Issues. (1948). *4*, 4. L. Meyerson (Ed.), The American Psychological Association. Boston Linotype Print, Inc. Boston: Mass.

Katz, I. , Farber, J., Glass, D., Lucido, D., and Emswiller, T. (1978). When courtesy offends: Effects of positive and negative behavior by the physically disabled on altruism and anger in normals. *Journal of Personality, 46.* 3, 506-518.

Katz, I. (1981). Stigma: *A social-psychological analysis*. Hillside, NJ. Erlbaum.

Kelly, G. (1955). *The psychology of personal constructs*. New York: North.

Kelly, H.H., Hastorf, A.H., Jones, E.E., Thibaut, J. W. and Usdane, W.M. (1960). *Some implications of social-psychological theory for research on the handicapped*. In Psychological Research and Rehabilitation. Miami Conference Report: American Psychological Association.

Kerlinger, F. (1973). *Foundations of behavioral research*. Second edition. Holt, Hinehart and Winston, Inc. New York.

Kim, Young Y. (1988). *Communication and cross-cultural adaptation: An integrative theory*. Avon, England: Multilingual Matters.

Kim, Young Y. (1989). Intercultural adaptation. *In handbook of international and intercultural communication*. Asante, M.K. and Gudykunst, W.B. (Eds.). Newbury Park, Calif. Sage.

Kitsuse, J.I. (1980). Coming out all over: Deviants and the politics of social problems. *Social Problems, 28*, (1), 1-12, (October).

Kleck, R., Ono, H., and Hastorf, A. (1966). The effects of physical deviance upon face-to-face interaction. *Human Relations, 19*, 425-436.

Kleck, R. (1968). Physical stigma and nonverbal cues emitted in face-to-face interaction. *Human Relations, 21*, 19-28.

Kleck, R. (1969). Physical stigma and task oriented interaction. *Human Relations, 22*, 53-59.

Klopf, W.D. (1987). *Intercultural encounters: The fundamentals of intercultural communication*. Morton Publishing Co.

Kluckholn, F. and Strodtbeck, F. (1961). *In building communication theory*. Infante, D.A; Rancer, S.A; Womack, D.F. (1990). Waveland Press, Inc.

Kohlberg, L. (1969). *Stages and Sequence: The cognitive-developmental approach to socialization.* In D. Goslin (Ed.), Handbook of socialization theory and research (347-480). Chicago: Rand McNally.

Kojima, Y. (1977). Disabled individuals in Japanese society. *Rehabilitation World, 3*, 18-19 and 22-25.

Kroeber, A.L. and Kluckholn, C. (1952). Culture: A critical review of concepts and definitions. In Donald W. Klopf (Ed.), *Intercultural encounters: The fundamentals of intercultural communications.* Morton Publishing Company, Englewood, Colorado.

Kuhn, T.S. (1970). *The structure of scientific revolutions.* Chicago: University of Chicago Press.

Kushel, R. (1973). The silent inventor: The creation of a sign language by the only deaf-mute on a Polynesian island. *Sign Language Studies, 3*, 1-28.

Ladieu, G.L., Adler, D.L. and Dembo, T. (1948). Studies in adjustment to visible injuries: Social acceptance of the injured. In L. Meyerson (Ed.), *Journal of Social Issues, 4*, 4, 55-61.

Langer, E.J., Fiske, S., Taylor, S.E., and Chanovitz, B. (1976). Stigma, staring and discomfort: A novel stimulus hypothesis. *Journal of Experimental Social Psychology, 12*, 451-463.

Leavitt, R. (1992). *Disability and rehabilitation in rural Jamaica. An ethnographic study.* Rutherford, Madison and Teaneck. Fairleigh.

Lincoln, Y. and Guba, E. (1985). *Naturalistic Inquiry.* Sage: California.

Lindlof, T.R. (1995). *Qualitative communication research methods.* Current Communication: An advanced text series, 3.

Littlejohn, S. (1992). *Theories of intercultural communication.* Wadsworth Publishing Co. Belmont, CA.

Lowman, C.L. and Seidenfield, M.A. (1947). Psychosocial effects of poliomyelitis. *Journal of Consulting Psychology, 11,* 30.

Makas, E. (1988). Positive attitudes toward disabled people: Disabled and nondisabled persons' perspectives. *Journal of Social Issues, 44.* 1, 49-61.

Manley, M. (1990). *The politics of change: A Jamaican testament.* Howard University Press: Washington D.C.

Maslow, A.H. (1943). A theory of human motivation. <u>Psychological Review,</u> 50. In Donald W. Klopf (Ed.), *Intercultural encounters: The fundamentals of intercultural communications.* Morton Publishing Company, Englewood: Colorado.

McAndrew, H. (1948). Rigidity in the deaf and the blind. *Journal of Social Issues, 4.* 4, 72-77.

McCaskill-Emerson, C. (1992). *It's a black deaf thing.* A paper presented at a conference at the Model Secondary School for the Deaf. Washington, D.C. July 30, 1992.

McGrath, J.E. (1980). What are the social issues? Timeliness and treatment of topics in the Journal of Social Issues. *Journal of Social Issues, 36,* 4, 98-108.

McNeil, J.M. (1983). *Labor force and other characteristics of persons with a work disability: 1982* (Series p-23, No. 127). Washington, D.C.: U.S. Bureau of the Census.

Merriam, A. (1974). *An African world: The Besongye.* Bloomington: Indiana University Press.

Mest, G. M. (1988). With a little help from their friends: Use of social support systems by persons with retardation. *Journal of Social Issues, 44.* 1, 117-125.

Meyerson, L. (1948a). Experimental injury: An approach to the dynamics of disability. In L. Meyerson (Ed.), *Journal of Social Issues, 4,* 4, 68-71.

Meyerson, L. (1948b). Physical disability as a social psychological problem. In L. Meyerson (Ed.), *Journal of Social Issues, 4,* 4, 2-9.

Meyerson, L. (1948c). The social psychology of physical disability. In L. Meyerson (Ed.), *Journal of Social Issues, 4,* 4, 103-105.

Meyerson, L. (1948d). A fair employment act for the disabled. In L. Meyerson (Ed.), *Journal of Social Issues, 4,* 4, 107-109.

Meyerson, L. (1948e). Social action for the disabled. In L. Meyerson (Ed.), *Journal of Social Issues, 4,* 4, 11-112.

Meyerson, L., Gonick, M. R., Wright, B.A.,Barker, R.G. (1953). *Adjustment to physical handicap and illness: A survey of the social psychology of physique and disability.* (2nd Ed.). New York: Social Science Research Council.

Meyerson, L. (1988). The social psychology of physical disability.: 1948-1988. *Journal of Social Issues, 44,* 1, 173-188.

Murdock, G.P. (1956). How culture changes. In H.L. Shapiro (Ed.), *Man, Culture and Society.* New York: Oxford University Press.

Murphy, R.F., Scheer, J., Murphy, Y., and Mack, R. (1988). Physical disability and social liminality: A study in the rituals of adversity. *Social Science and Medicine, 26,* 1, 235-242.

Mwaria, C. B. (1990). The concept of self in the context of crisis: A study of families of the severely brain-injured. *Social Science Medicine, 30.* 8, 889-893.

Nagi, S. Z. (1981). The concept and measurement of disability. *Annual Review of Rehabilitation, 2.* New York. Springer.

New, P. K-M. (1984). Disability research and policy. *Social Science Medicine, 19,* 6, 585-586.

Nicotera, A.M. (1993). Beyond two dimensions: A grounded theory model of conflict-handling behavior. *Management Communication Quarterly,* 6, 3, 282-306.

Nirje, B. (1976). The normalization principle. In Kugel, R.B. and Shearer, A. (Eds.). *Changing patterns in residential services for the mentally retarded* (revised edition). Washington, D.C.: President's Committee on Mental Retardation, 231.

Novak, P.W. and Lerner, M.J. (1968). Rejection as a consequence of perceived similarity. *Journal of Personality and Social Psychology, 9,* 147-152.

Pearce, B.W. and Cronen V. (1980). *Communication Action and Meaning.* New York: Praeger.

Pearson, J. C. (1984). The challenge of helping the handicapped. *Social Science Medicine, 19,* 6, 587-588.

Perry, H.S., Gawel, M.L., and Gibbon, M. (Eds.), (1956): *Clinical Studies in Psychiatry,* New York: W.W. Norton and Company.

Phillips, M.J. (1985). "Try harder": The experience of disability and the dilemma of normalization. *The Social Science Journal, 22.* 4, 45-57.

Phillips, M. J. (1990). Damaged goods: Oral narratives of the experience of disability in American culture. *Social Science Medicine, 30.* 8, 849-857.

Plank, E.N. and Horwood, C. (1961). Leg amputation in a four year old. *Psychoanalytic Study of the Child, 16.* pp. 405-422. International University Press, Inc. N.Y.: N.Y.

Pope, C. R. (1984). Disability and health status: The importance of longitudinal studies. *Social Science Medicine, 19,* 6, 589-593.

Prosser, M.H. (1978). The cultural dialogue: *An introduction to intercultural communication.* Boston: Houghton Mifflin.

Richardson, S.A., Hastorf, A.H., Goodman N and Dornbusch S.M. (1961). Cultural uniformity in reaction to physical disabilities. *American Sociolical Review, 26,* 241-247.

Rosman, A. (1962). *Social structure and acculturation among the Kanuri of Northern Nigeria.* Unpublished doctoral dissertation. Yale University.

Rothman, D. (1971). *The discovery of the asylum: Social order and disorder in the new republic*. Boston: Little, Brown.

Rubin, Z. and Peplau, L. (1975). Who believes in a just world? *Journal of Social Issues, 31*, 65-89.

Rusk, H.A., and Taylor, E.J. (1948). Employment for the disabled. In L. Meyerson (Ed.), *Journal of Social Issues. 4*, 4, 101-105.

Sagatun, I.J. (1985). The effects of acknowledging a disability and initiating contact on interaction between disabled and non-disabled persons. *The Social Science Journal, 22*, 4, 33-43.

Scheer, J. and Groce, N. (1988). Impairment as a human constant: Cross-cultural and historical perspectives on variation. *Journal of Social Issues, 44*, 1, 23-37.

Schneider, J. (1988). Disability as moral experience; Epilepsy and self in routine relationships. *Journal of Social Issues, 44*, 1, 63-78.

Schneider, J. W., and Conrad, P. (1980). In the closet with illness: *Epilepsy, stigma potential and information control, 28*, 1, 32-44.

Schroedel, J.G. (1984). Analyzing surveys on deaf adults: Implications for survey research on persons with disabilities. *Social Science Medicine, 19*, 6, 619-627.

Schulz, R. and Decker, S. (1985). Long term adjustment to physical disability: The role of social support, perceived control, and self blame. *Journal of Personality and Social Psychology, 48*, 1162-1172.

Scotch, R. K. (1988). Disability as the basis for a social movement.: Advocacy and the politics of definition. *Journal of Social Issues, 44*, 1, 159-172.

Seidman, E. (1986). Justice, values, and social science: Unexamined premises. In E. Seidman and J. Rappaport (Eds.), *Redefining social problems*, 235-258. New York: Plenum.

Shimanoff, S. (1980). *Communication rules: Theory and research*. Beverly Hills, Calif.: Sage.

Shontz, F.C. (1977). Six principles relating to disability and psychological adjustment. *Rehabilitation Psychology, 24*, 207-210.

Shuman, M. (1980). The sounds of silence in Noyha: A preliminary account of sign language use by the deaf in a Maya community in Yucatan, Mexico. *Language Sciences, 2,* 144-173.

Smith, A. G. (1966). *Communication and Culture*. New York: Holt, Rinehart and Winston.

Smith, M.J. (1982). Cognitive schemata and persuasive communication: Toward a contingency rules theory. In *Communication yearbook 6*. Beverly Hills, Calif.: Sage.

Solnit, A.J. and Stark, M.H. (1961). Mourning the birth of a defective child. *The Psychoanalytic Study of the Child, 16*, 523-537.

Solomon, H.M.(1986). Stigma and western culture: A historical approach. In S. Ainlay, G. Becker, and L. Coleman (Eds.). *The dilemma of difference: A multidisciplinary view of stigma*, 59-67. New York, Plenuum.

Stewart, D. W. and Shamdasani, P.N. (1990). Focus Groups: Theory and Practice. *Applied Social Research Methods Series, 20*, Sage Publications. Newbury Park. London. New Delhi.

Stone, D. (1984). *The disabled state*. Philadelphia: Temple University Press.

Sussman, J. (1994). Disability, stigma and deviance. *Social Science Medicine, 38*, 1, 15-22.

Taylor, S.E., Wood, J.V., and Lichtman, R.R. (1983). It could be worse: selective evaluation as a response to victimization. *Journal of Social Issues, 39*, 2, 19-40.

Tenny, J. W. (1953). The minority status of the handicapped. *Exceptional Children, 19*, 260-264.

Thompson, T.L. (1981). The development of communication skills in physically handicapped children. *Human Communication Research, 7.* 4, 312-324.

Thompson, T.L. (1982). Gaze toward, and avoidance of the handicapped: A field experiment. *Journal of Nonverbal Behavior, 6,* 3, 188-196.

Thorburn, M.J. (1993a). *Report of a survey of knowledge, attitudes, and practices in three areas in Jamaica in 1993.* Department of Social and Preventive Medicine, University of the West Indies, Mona, Kingston 7, Jamaica.

Thorburn, M.J. (1993b). *The situation of disabled children in Jamaica.* A report compiled for Unicef. Department of Social and Preventive Medicine, University of the West Indies, Mona, Kingston 7, Jamaica.

Thorburn, M.J., Desai, P., and Paul, T.J. (1992c). Service needs of children with disabilities in Jamaica. *International Journal of Rehabilitation Research, 15,* 31-38.

Turner, V. (1967). *The forest of symbols: Aspects of Ndembu ritual.* Cornell University Press, Ithaca, N.Y.

Turner, V. (1969). *The ritual process: Structure and anti-structure.* Cornell University Press, Ithaca, N.Y.

Ungar, S. (1979). The effects of effort and stigma on helping. *The Journal of Social Psychology, 107,* 1, 23-28.

van Cleve J.V. and Crouch, B.A. (1989). *A place of their own: Creating the deaf community in America.* Gallaudet University Press. Washington, D.C.

Vernon, M. (1983). Foreword. In Hairston, E. and Smith, L. (1983). *Black and Deaf in America: Are we that different?*

von Hentig, H. (1948). Physical desirability, mental conflict and social crisis. *Journal of Social Issues, 4,* 4, 21-27.

Wafer, L. (1934). *A new voyage and description of the isthmus of America.* Oxford, England: Hakluyt Society.

Weinberg-Asher, N. (1976). The effects of physical disability on self-perception. *Rehabilitation Counseling Bulletin, 20,* 1, 15-20.

Weiss, C. H. (1980). Knowledge creep and decision accretion. *Knowledge: creation, diffusion, utilization, 1,* 381-404.

Weiss, S. (1985). *Cross-cultural patterns of disability in non-Western societies.* Unpublished honors paper. Department of Anthropology, Brown University.

Williams, V. (1918). *The man with the clubfoot.* Jenkins: London.

Wilson, E.D. and Alcorn, D. (1969). Disability, simulation and development of attitudes toward the exceptional. *Journal of Special Education, 3,* 3, 305-307.

Wolf, A. (1981). *Taking the quantum leap.* San Francisco: Harper and Row.

World program of action for disabled people. January 1983-December 1992. United Nations: New York.

Wright, B.A., White, R.K. & Dembo, T. (1948). Studies in adjustment to visible injuries: Evaluation of curiosity by the injured. *Journal of Abnormal and Social Psychology, 43,* 13-28.

Wright, B.A. (1960). *Physical disability: A psychological approach.* New York: Harper and Row.

Wright, B.A. (1983). *Physical disability: A psychosocial approach.* New York: Harper and Row.

Wyatt v. Stickney 3195 US 3 1972

Zola, K.I. (1985). Depictions of disability-metaphor, message, and medium in the media: A research and political agenda. *The Social Science Journal, 22,* 4, 5-17.

Zola, K.I. (1993). Self, identity and the naming question: Reflections on the language of disability. *Social Science Medicine, 36,* 2, 167-173.

Author Index

132

Granofsky, J.
Groce, N.
Guba, E.
Gudykunst, W.B.

Hahn, H.
Hairston, E.
Hall, E.T.
Hanks, J.R.
Hanks, L.M.
Hardaway, B.
Hastorf, A.H.
Hecht, M.L.
Hess, M.
Higgins, P.C.
Hofstede, G.
Holy Bible, King James Version
Homans, G.L.
Horowitz, I.
Horwood, C.
Infante, D.A.

Jacques, M.E.
Jankowski, K.
Johnson, R.C.
Jones, E.E.
Journal of Social Issues
Karuza, J.
Katz, I.
Kelly, G.
Kelly, H.H.
Kerlinger, F.
Kidler, L.
Kim, Young Y.
Kitsuse, J.I.
Kleck, R.
Klopf, W.D.
Kluckholn, C.
Kohlberg, L.
Kojima, Y.
Kroeber, A.L.
Kuhn, T.S.
Ladieu, G.L.
Langer, E.J.
Leavitt, R.
Lerner, M.J.
Liebowitz, M
Lincoln, Y
Lindlof, T.R.
Linkowski, D.C.
Litchman, R.R.
Littlejohn, S.

Lucido, D.
Lowman, C.L.

Makas, E.
Manley, M.
Markus, H.
Maslow, A.H.
McAndrew, H.
McCaskill-Emerson, C.
McGrath, J.E.
McNeil, J.M.

Merriam, A.
Mest, G.M.
Meyerson, L.
Miller, D.T.
Murdock, G.P.
Murphey, R.F.
Murphy, Y.
Mwaria, C.B.

Nagi, S.Z.
New, P. K-M.
Nicotera, A.M.
Nirje, B.
Novak, P.W.

Ono, H.

Pearce, B.W.
Pearson, J.C.
Peplau, L.
Perry, H.S.
Phillips, M.J.
Plank, E.N.
Pope, C.R.
Prosser, M.H.

Rabonovitz, V.C.
Rancer, S.A.
Ribeau, S.A.
Richard, M.
Richardson, S.A.
Rubin, Z.
Rusk, H.A.

Sagatun, I.J.
Scheer, J.
Scneider, J.W.
Scott, R.A.
Schulz, R.
Scotch, R.K.

Subject Index

136